The Racer's Edge

The Racer's Edge

Memoirs of an Isle of Man TT Legend

DAVE MOLYNEUX

with Matthew Richardson

Wharncliffe Books

First published in Great Britain in 2011 by
Wharncliffe
an imprint of
Pen & Sword Books Ltd
47 Church Street
Barnsley
South Yorkshire
S70 2AS

ISBN 978-1-84563-142-0

Typeset in 11pt Ehrhardt by
Mac Style, Beverley, E. Yorkshire

Printed and bound in India by Replika Press Pvt. Ltd.

Pen & Sword Books Ltd incorporates the imprints of Pen & Sword
Aviation, Pen & Sword Maritime, Pen & Sword Military, Wharncliffe
Local History, Pen & Sword Select, Pen & Sword Military Classics,
Leo Cooper, Seaforth Publishing and Frontline Publishing.

For a complete list of Pen & Sword titles please contact
PEN & SWORD BOOKS LIMITED
47 Church Street, Barnsley, South Yorkshire, S70 2AS, England
E-mail: enquiries@pen-and-sword.co.uk
Website: www.pen-and-sword.co.uk

Contents

List of Illustrations

Myself and brother Graham in our film debut.
In pole position for the Dutch round of the European Championship, at Assen in March 1995.
In action at the 1995 Ulster Grand Prix.
Racing in the Czech Republic at the Most circuit, 1995.
On the podium after victory in the Sidecar B race, 1996 TT.
Waiting for the start at Schleiz.
Racing in the wet at Schleiz, 1996.
August 1996: winners at the European Championship round at Schleiz, Germany.
Racing in the 1996 Czech Grand Prix at Brno.
The machine in Honda Britain colours for the 1998 TT.
Looking pleased after victory in the 1998 Sidecar TT.
Myself and Craig Hallam testing at Jurby airfield before the 1999 TT.
In action during the Sidecar World Cup, 2000.
2002 at the TT and back with Colin Hardman in the chair.
In action in Honda colours during the 2002 TT.
A classic TT image: coming down off the mountain at Creg-ny-Baa, 2004.
2006: in practice for the TT.
On the final lap, 1 June 2006.
The 2006 crash: the aftermath.
In practice for the 2007 Centenary TT.
Myself and Kenny Arthur, following the 2007 TT parade lap.
With Terry Windle at the 2007 TT.
In the colours of Peter Lloyd Racing for the 2007 Superside series.
The machine in Suzuki colours for the 2008 TT.
Dan Sayle and myself, Suzuki-powered again at the 2009 TT.
Myself and passenger Patrick Farrance in the 2010 TT.
The 2010 machine stripped down to the chassis.

Acknowledgements

The authors would like to express their appreciation towards a number of people for their help in the preparation of this book. First and foremost our thanks must go to our families for their patience and understanding while the book was being compiled, and also for their advice and encouragement.

A great many people have provided photographs, and we would like to thank in particular Dave Collister for his generosity in providing a selection of his fantastic shots for inclusion in this book. More of Dave's work can be found on his website www.photocycles.com, and in his recently published book *Shutter Speed*.

Eric Whitehead likewise searched his archives to help us fill gaps in the photographic record, and very kindly allowed the use of a number of his images. Alwyn Collister generously supplied photographs which he took during practice for the 2006 TT.

František Feigl in the Czech Republic contributed a marvellous photograph from the 1995 European Championships. Dieter Fleischer in Germany allowed us to use a number of his photographs taken at the Schleiz circuit, for which we are most grateful, and Roger Lohrer provided that taken at Hockenheim. Simon Crellin at Redpoint PR was also most helpful in supplying photos from the Isle of Man TT Press Office for use in the book.

Special thanks must go to Matthew Barney, for permission to use a still from the film *Cremaster 4*, and also to the staff of the Gladstone Gallery, New York, in particular Sascha Crasnow, for their helpfulness.

Finally it would be impossible to overstate the contribution made by John Caley. John took a number of original photographs for our use, and also provided the excellent technical drawings herein. Unfortunately it was not possible to trace all copyright holders, though extensive efforts were made to contact all identifiable photographers whose work has been used in this book.

Peter Richardson read the early draft and offered many comments and improvements, for which we thank him. We would also like to thank Rupert Harding at Pen & Sword Books for his enthusiasm and support for this project right from the very beginning. The design staff at Pen & Sword are also to be congratulated, as always, on a first-class piece of work.

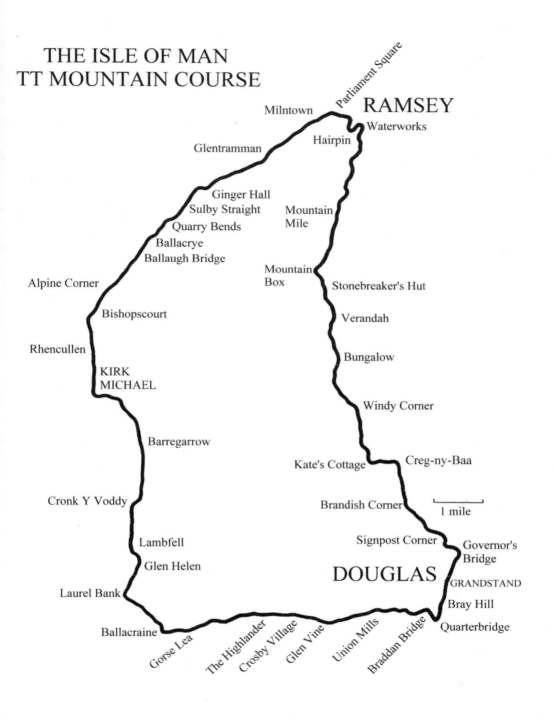

THE ISLE OF MAN
TT MOUNTAIN COURSE

Parliament Square

RAMSEY

Milntown

Waterworks

Hairpin

Glentramman

Ginger Hall

Sulby Straight

Mountain Mile

Quarry Bends

Ballacrye

Ballaugh Bridge

Mountain Box

Alpine Corner

Stonebreaker's Hut

Bishopscourt

Verandah

Rhencullen

Bungalow

KIRK MICHAEL

Windy Corner

Barregarrow

Creg-ny-Baa

Kate's Cottage

Cronk Y Voddy

Brandish Corner

1 mile

Lambfell

Signpost Corner

Governor's Bridge

Glen Helen

DOUGLAS

Laurel Bank

GRANDSTAND

Bray Hill

Ballacraine

Quarterbridge

Gorse Lea

The Highlander

Crosby Village

Glen Vine

Union Mills

Braddan Bridge

Introduction

The 37¾-mile Isle of Man Tourist Trophy (TT) mountain circuit is widely recognized as the toughest motor racing venue anywhere in the world. Originally conceived as a test of endurance for road-going motorcycles, the now legendary Tourist Trophy races were first run in 1907 and are still reckoned to be among the hardest of any on racing machinery. If a motorcycle can survive the unique rigours of the Isle of Man's mountain circuit, it can survive anywhere. Coupled with this, the course (an otherwise ordinary set of roads in use throughout the year) presents unique challenges to the rider. It climbs from 100 feet above sea level to nearly 2,000 feet at its highest point. The course is lined with trees, telegraph poles, stone walls and houses, meaning that the margins for error vary from slight to non-existent.

Two things make the Isle of Man TT an unparalleled event. One is the unique atmosphere on the Island during two weeks in May and June each year, when biking enthusiasts from across the world gather on this tiny patch of earth. In 2006 *MotorCycle News* described the TT as the 'number one must-see' event in the annual motorcycling calendar, ahead of the British round of Moto GP and World Superbikes. The second factor in the equation is the sheer weight of motorcycling heritage which this event possesses, encapsulated by the spectacular series of silver mercury trophies for which riders compete. The TT mountain course is the oldest motorcycle racing circuit in the world which is still in use, and commentating legend Murray Walker has stated in the past that no other comparable motorsport event has as much history as does the Isle of Man TT.

Motorcycle and sidecar combinations have competed in this arena in two distinct phases. The first, from 1922 to 1929, ended because of pressure from manufacturers. They felt that sidecar racing was not helping their image as a reliable and safe means of family transport, an image which at the time they were trying to promote. The second phase began with the reintroduction of sidecar racing in 1955, and continues to the present day. This branch of motor sport is in many ways unique. Unlike any other form of motorcycle racing, driver and passenger must work closely as a team. The passenger must display great ability as he shifts his weight around to ensure maximum adhesion of the tyres on the track. In terms of sheer spectacle, there is little to compete with modern sidecar racing. The machines themselves have altered much from their early antecedents. The frame of the bike has become low and squat. The tyres have become much wider than those of a standard motorcycle in order to increase grip. The rider (or driver as he is frequently described) usually adopts a kneeling, rather than sitting position.

The 1950s saw British stars such as Eric Oliver shine in the sidecar TT, but both this decade and the 1960s were dominated by German competitors, mainly on BMW outfits. In the 1970s, the German dominance of the event was broken to a certain extent with the emergence of British competitors such as George O'Dell, Sidecar World Champion in 1977, and Jock Taylor, who was World Champion in 1980. While the loss of World Championship status in 1976 saw the TT decline in importance for solo machinery, the change had the opposite effect upon the sidecar classes. Today it could be argued that the sidecar events at the Isle of Man TT represent the pinnacle of that sport in Great Britain. For many years now the *force majeure* at the TT has been Dave Molyneux, a man who has, largely through his perseverance and dedication, come to dominate the event. Molyneux is one of the most prolific sidecar racers in British history. His racing career has spanned an incredible thirty-one years. His tally of fourteen TT wins makes him not only the most successful sidecar competitor in the history of the event, but also the most successful Manx competitor and joint third most successful competitor ever with Mike Hailwood, after Joey Dunlop and John McGuinness. He has also competed in the British Sidecar Championships, Grand Prix races and other international events.

His natural talent and ability as a sidecar driver, together with his ambition and hunger for success, have been proved again and again on race tracks around the world. His will to succeed and to overcome problems has been blunted neither by racing injuries nor by financial difficulties. However, Molyneux has carved out an equally impressive reputation as a constructor, and his machines are in demand in the racing world. Molyneux is also perhaps one of the more controversial figures in British motorcycle racing. Sometimes outspoken, and often forthright in his views, he believes in speaking what is on his mind. Undoubtedly, his views have at times earned him unpopularity in the paddock, while his need to achieve total concentration before a race and his steely determination to win have earned him the nickname 'Moody Moly' among certain commentators. A complex character, his outlook on life and racing has been coloured by personal tragedies and circumstances.

Two milestones in the production of this book remain fixed in my mind. The first took place one bright Friday morning in the early summer of 2006; I was listening to the radio in my kitchen, when breakfast-time news announced that during the previous evening's practice session, sidecar TT favourite and current lap record holder Dave Molyneux had been seriously injured in a high-speed crash. His machine had been burned out in the catastrophic accident and as a result Molyneux himself had announced from his hospital bed his decision to abandon racing. The career of the Isle of Man's most remarkable and prolific TT competitor appeared to be over.

Prior to that point, my contact with Dave Molyneux had been limited to a couple of phone calls, and although I had followed his career with some degree of interest I knew little about the man himself or what inspired him. A couple of weeks later and quite unexpectedly I had another call from Molyneux. He had a number of things he wanted to discuss with me, and invited me to his home in Regaby. This was the second milestone! Moly had been mulling over the question of what to do with his fire-damaged sidecar. This completely self-built outfit had won three TT races and smashed the lap record twice. Rather than attempt to rebuild it, he had decided instead to offer this historic machine to the Manx Museum. I was impressed by his appreciation of the importance of the heritage which surrounds the TT races, and which draws visitors annually from across the world, and fascinated as the story of what had inspired him unfolded. It subsequently became clear as we chatted that he had not after all decided to quit racing, and indeed that the Molyneux story was far from over. I really felt the sensation that day that here I was in the presence of someone who had not only made TT history but was actually *still* making it. It turned out that I wasn't wrong. Molyneux bounced back from that potentially career-ending crash to take centre stage at the 2007 Centenary TT, and in front of the biggest crowd the Island had seen in a quarter of a century, won both of the sidecar races.

Two things ultimately stemmed from that Regaby meeting. The first was that this historic machine eventually became part of the collections of Manx National Heritage, preserved for posterity as a lasting visual testament to this remarkable man's engineering ability and achievement. The second was that the more I found out about Molyneux himself, the more fascinated I became. Occasionally history produces men whose steely determination (and indeed physical bravery) propels them forward to achieve great things against overwhelming odds. Such men are often more respected than liked – think of men such as Guy Gibson and Douglas Bader to name but two – and I could see interesting parallels here with Molyneux. I became determined to persuade him to set out his story in a published book, as an accompanying written record. What happened next is what you are about to read: the story … so far!

Matthew Richardson

Chapter 1

Cutting My Teeth

Some people say that a thing is in their blood; well, in my case racing sidecars really is in mine. I was born in Douglas on the Isle of Man, in the Jane Crookall Maternity Home to be precise, on 21 November 1963. I grew up at Glen Maye, on the outskirts of Patrick, in the west of the Island. I was the oldest of six children of John and Joan Molyneux. There was myself, Kevin, Judy, Georgina, Graham and Allan. My mother and father bought a house in Kirk Michael when I was about three years old, called Tower House. It was a hectic home, really hectic. There always seemed to be babies and kids around throughout my early life; I grew up with it. I guess I felt it was a pain in the ass growing up with all the screaming and kids running around.

My dad was a motor mechanic, he started sidecar racing when I was two years old. That, I suppose, is why I've got an obsession with it. I was in it, with it and loved it straight away. My earliest memories are of workshops and more especially of going away to race events. My father raced with a guy called Ernie Leece from Peel, they were very successful together; they did well at the TT and got a third place in 1970, and I remember going away with them as early as four or five years old to Oulton Park, places like that, and seeing all the old pudding-basin helmets lined up on the pit wall. I've got vivid recollections of that kind of thing – I took it home with me, took it to bed with me even! When I was a kid I would lie down beside my trike and pretend to be a passenger on a sidecar. Motorbikes were it as far as I was concerned. I remember when I started school at Kirk

Michael Primary at four years old, I recall kicking and screaming like mad on the first day, and the headmaster carrying me in, and sitting me in the corner with a load of motorbike books, because he knew that was what I was into; he knew all my family were, at any rate. So there was me, happy for the rest of the day. I've still got one of my early school books. I must have been about six or seven when I wrote in it, 'At the weekend we played sidecars, I made the sidecar and it went off like a bomb.' Years later that page from my exercise book was used by Honda as an illustration in one of their souvenir booklets. Even at that young age I was obsessed with building and racing sidecars. But I never really liked school, and the more it went on the more I hated it. At ten or eleven years old, I'd skive off school at any given opportunity, sometimes going to work with my dad. In the late 1970s my dad teamed up and raced with another sidecar driver called George Oates. Every Wednesday night after work or school, dad and I would go to George Oates's house on the Ballamoda Straight to work on the sidecar. We also spent the day there every Sunday working on the outfit – Sunday was sidecar day – I was friends with George's son Howard and he and I used to have great fun, riding on our bikes.

When I got to ten years old, my mum and dad started going through some real difficult times and I was aware of that, I could see it all happening and going wrong. The last thing I wanted was to see them split, but they did, inevitably, and me and all my brothers and sisters went with my mum. My mum and dad got back together some months later, until one day during the summer holidays. My dad and I were up at four o'clock in the morning and off to work, and my mum would never get up and see us out to the door at that time of the morning. But this particular morning she was, and she was crying, and I thought, 'Oh no, something's going on here.' At six o'clock that evening – fourteen hours later, and my dad must have been sitting on this all that time – we were driving through the Devil's Elbow on the coast road back to Kirk Michael, and my dad turned and said to me,

'Look, David, I've got some news,' and I could tell by his voice there was shit going on, and I said, 'Is she gone, dad?' – I came straight out with it – and he replied, 'Yeah, she's packed and gone.' I just answered, 'Well, we'll manage, won't we?' and that was that. I went to live with my father then. He was my hero, and because I'd felt so strongly about their first split, I think they must have talked it over and decided that I was going to live with my dad from now on. I looked on us as best pals, not dad and son. But as a result of the split we moved out of Tower House, which is still to this day my favourite home of all the places that I've lived in.

Another of my earliest memories was of being at the TT with my dad in 1976, and watching George O'Dell.[1] My father was competing, actually, and I went up into the Grandstand to watch him in the Thursday afternoon practice session. I remember there was a yellow and green bike, with number 2 on it, bloody *shrieking* past! They had no silencers on them or anything like that in those days, and this bike did three laps that afternoon, the driver simulated a race on that practice session. I didn't have a programme and I didn't know who number 2 was. My only thought was, 'Jesus, this thing is *incredible.*' This bike, the noise of it, how it looked, everything about it was in another world. It just blew me away, and when my dad came in from practice all hot and sweaty, puffing and panting, and I ran up to him and said, 'Dad', he must have thought, 'Oh, the young fella's all excited to see me.' Instead I straight away asked him, 'Who's number 2 with the yellow and green bike?' and he just muttered back, 'Uh, that'll be O'Dell'! That was it then, I read every newspaper article, every interview with him that I could find, and I just followed him. In 1977 I actually met O'Dell – his machine was in yellow and red livery that year because his sponsor had changed now from BP to Shell – and one night during TT practice week he was testing on the Ballamoda Straight. Riders weren't supposed to do that, because it was just an ordinary stretch of road, but lots of them did in those days! He wasn't the only one there that night; Phil Read was there as well, letting rip up and down with one of the solo bikes which he rode at the TT that year. I was at George Oates's house that night and we heard the sidecar roaring up and down. Howard Oates, George's son, and myself were both big sidecar fans and we both rushed out to see what was happening. Howard and I got the chance to sit on the bike, and O'Dell's passenger Kenny Arthur took a photo of us, using my Box Brownie camera.

That year, 1977, my dad and George Oates were seventh in the first leg of the TT, and George O'Dell won that race. He went on to book his place in history that year because he went on from the TT to win the 1977 Sidecar World Championship. I can remember it like it was yesterday. I loved it not only because O'Dell won, and he was my hero back then, but also because my father and George Oates were right in the thick of it, they were dicing with British champions and World Championship contenders. At that time you could easily say they were the best of the rest, because they were on far inferior equipment compared to these other guys. I'm sure if they'd had that equipment they would have been level pegging, but they didn't and that was that. But it was a hell of an exciting period for me, to be so captivated by these guys – there was Rolf Steinhausen[2] and Rolf Biland,[3] people like that. It was the era when the oily British engines were just giving way to the sleek new Japanese motors which would dominate sidecar racing from then on, a classic age in many ways. In fact if I could have been born thirty years or so earlier, it would have been my dream to race on those kinds of machines against those people.

One day later that same year, and I remember being really hacked off about this, my dad told me, 'You're going to have to go and stay at your auntie's while I go to the Ulster Grand Prix,' and I said, 'Well, I don't get that, because I've gone to England racing with you, I've been everywhere racing with you, and you won't bloody take me to this!' It was like a real lover's spat, like me saying to the wife, 'You're not coming on this trip!' So I was real hacked off, but anyway I went to stay at my auntie's. I loved being there because it was up in Dalby where my dad grew up. I was staying with his brother; they had a huge family of eight kids, and it was great, like a big adventure playground.

So he dropped me off there, and I remember being really arsy and grumpy, and he said, 'Right, tara then,' and I don't think I even said 'tara' or goodbye to him. It sounds strange now, but while my dad was away I went shopping in Douglas with my Auntie Jen and I remember that I bought a keyring in one of the tourist shops with a picture of dad and George on it. Then I went to buy a small silver cup, the sort of thing you give on Father's Day, with 'World's Best Dad' on it. But I didn't buy it. I put it back down because for some reason that I can't explain I had a very bad feeling about it … Well, my auntie didn't have a phone, back then in 1977, and less than a week later the police came to the door. The news wasn't good: John's had a real bad accident, he's in Belfast Infirmary fighting for his life. I can remember them to this day, two policemen standing there, and I got called through, I remember my auntie was crying. Two days later he was dead. I didn't see him again; I didn't go over there to Belfast. Money was tight, and I suppose they thought I was too young to handle that sort of thing. He was on a life support machine, and he wasn't even aware of what was going on. George Oates, the driver of the bike, had died instantly. They kept my father alive for two days, but he had serious head injuries.

I was a real bad-tempered little bastard anyway in those days, and I think a lot of that stemmed from my mum and dad's split. But I remember being even more pissed off that I'd finally got myself into a good situation with my dad, and it had all just turned shite again with his death. I'd had a family, and then it had all been taken away from me. I had a lot of resentment, towards certain people and towards the whole situation. I was quite old for my years anyway – I think that stemmed from working with my dad, he worked with a load of blokes and it was all lads' stuff – so I knew full well what had been going on. As soon as the police left, and my auntie got her head together, my uncle got called back from the farm, but I just said, 'Look, I'm not going back to her house,' meaning my mum. I wanted to stay with them, and of course they were put in a bad position by this. Looking back, it must have been a nightmare for them to try and deal with. Anyway, my mum came up and after a lot of discussion I went back home with her but I did not like it one bit; that was the truth. Around this time I also remember my uncle telling me to get racing out of my head, and to stop being so stupid. I answered him back quite defiantly, saying that by the time I was twenty-five years old, I'd win the sidecar TT!

Some time later that year, at the invitation of the Andreas Racing Association, George O'Dell came over to the Isle of Man with his sidecar outfit. He did a benefit night at the Palace Lido in Douglas, to raise money for the families of Oates and Molyneux. He had printed a thousand posters reading 'World Sidecar Champion' with a picture of his bike, and had signed them all. He sold them for £1 each in aid of the two families during that benefit night, and shifted the whole lot. Andreas Racing Association was the club to which my father and George had belonged, and they had established something called the Oates and Molyneux Children's Fund. All on its own that little gesture by George raised a grand, to go into the kitty for us all in the future. I think that says a lot about O'Dell, and the kind of man he was, that he wasn't too big to do something like that, and he used his status as World Champion to help the families of others less fortunate in his sport.

When I was about thirteen my mum took me to a lawyer, because she and my dad had been in the middle of divorce proceedings when he died; the lawyer said, 'I'm sorry, but David can actually choose where he wants to be. He can go to his auntie or whatever.' So all of a sudden I had all these choices to deal with. At my dad's local pub in Ballaugh, the Leeming family, George and Gladys Leeming, they wanted to adopt me, and they wanted to take me on holiday. I'd never been on a holiday in my bloody life. At the same time, my auntie and uncle would have had to get an extension built on their house to get another bedroom to fit me in, and also my mum was desperate to have me back there, so I was getting all these options thrown at me and there was this bloody tug-of-war going on with me slapped in the middle with all the choices. I was told by a lawyer that I could make that choice; and I look back now and think, 'For Christ's sake, you don't give a thirteen-year-old a choice like that.' I started thinking about school, and my mates and where I'd grown up, Kirk Michael, and I opted to stay with my mum, in the end. But I think it changed me a lot. It turned me into a real little shite, and people must have found me really hard to deal with. I perhaps used situations to my advantage at that age, I don't know. I feel looking back I was probably a nightmare. My mum would say different, I expect! Kids tend to see things as black and white but looking back now, and with the wisdom of an adult, I know that my dad was perhaps as much to blame for the split as my mum. I do know that there were an awful lot of situations which a kid shouldn't be aware of or be a witness to, so it was an explosive three years really.

Not long after my fourteenth birthday I was on a skateboard going through Kirk Michael down the middle of the village; there were half a dozen of us, and I got scooped up by a car; I went over the bonnet, then over the bloody roof. I broke my ankle, and gashed myself to bits! It was right outside our house that this happened, so my mum came running out, saying, 'Jesus Christ!' It was actually Rob Brew, who went to school with my mum and dad, who was driving. He's a real nice bloke who helps me out a bit still with the racing today, but the poor guy must have got the shock of his life when he saw a bunch of bloody kids skateboarding down the main road. I was at the tail end of it and was the one who got knocked over. When I say that I used certain situations to my advantage, that incident was one of them. Jesus, I broke my ankle true enough, but three days after I broke it Dr Brownsdon, the family doctor, said, 'He'll be right to go back to school.' I didn't go back for about eight weeks! All I needed to do was tell my mum it was too sore. 'Ah well, you can stay off,' she'd say, and that was it! She got in a bit of bother with that, I suppose, with the school, but then I got to my final year at school where I just could not be arsed. I've still got all my schoolwork from Ramsey Grammar School and I think for my final year I produced two pieces of paper with three lines of writing on, that's about all I did. The only subject I really enjoyed was art, because basically the art teachers were happy enough to let me draw whatever I wanted, even if it was sidecars. I've still got a few of those sketches I produced at school. Quite often I drew myself as passenger, like my dad had been, though as time went on I became more determined to be a sidecar driver. When my dad and George Oates were racing together, it was often talked about that Howard, George's son, would soon be racing, and young Moly would be on the side with him, as a new Oates and Molyneux combination. But once I got into doing my own thing I realized I was a driver, not a passenger and I've never passengered anybody to this day, it just doesn't interest me.

Well, we got to the end of our third year of school, before we started our final year, and I was then old enough to leave the following Easter if I wanted to. Me and a bunch of others about my age were told that if we wanted to leave that coming Easter, we would have to produce proof of a job that we were going on to. On my first day off in the summer holiday before my final year, I went straight into Peel, to Empire Garage, to see a guy called Dicky Craine who used to be my dad's boss. My dad had worked for him for a few years, and I said, 'I just wondered if I could have an apprenticeship at some point?' He answered, 'Yes, we'll be taking some apprentices on, when were you thinking?' When I said, 'Next Easter', he spluttered, 'Jesus Christ, I thought you meant at the end of the summer holidays or something!' I explained, 'Oh no, I need this job to come into, and I need proof of it, so can you give me a letter …' He told me that if I waited, he would type me one out there and then. So I was as happy as Larry after that.

The first day back at school, in September, I went straight to the headmaster's office, and produced this letter. He said, 'My word, David, you really want to leave, don't you?' I said, 'Damn right I do!'

So I left that Easter, and there was a little bit of money due to me from my dad's insurance. I think each of his children got, from memory, £500, put into a bank account. Some of the money from the Andreas Racing Association fund for the Oates and Molyneux children also went into that account. I was allowed to have mine hauled out early, I suppose this would be about two weeks before I left school. Then I went on a Saturday morning ferry on my own to Liverpool, and from a phone box I arranged to meet this guy who was advertising a sidecar outfit for sale in the *MotorCycle News*. I bought this bike from him on the dockside for £450. I had it in my top pocket, and in 1979 £450 in your top pocket was a fair old wad of money, especially for a lad of sixteen! But I took it over, met the guy, and bought the outfit. I pushed it up the ramp onto the car deck, with the help of some of the guys who worked on the boat. When I got off the other side I'd arranged for someone to give me a tow, and we towed it on a rope from Douglas docks down to Kirk Michael! The weird thing about all that, looking back on it now, was that some of that money at least would have come from the fund George O'Dell raised for us when he came to the Palace Lido that night in 1977, so in another way O'Dell was influential in getting me into sidecar racing.

The fact that my father had been killed racing sidecars had not put me off the sport; actually, it had probably made me more determined to succeed. I'm such a stubborn bastard and have been since birth, it probably just made me that much more single-minded. I was deeply upset by his death at the time, and if I'm truthful I still am now, but it drove me on more than it did anything else. I remember that when I started, it was bloody hard, and without that driving me, I might well have just given up. I was sixteen, and I didn't even know how to ride a road bike; to this day I've never had one, I've never passed a road-bike test, but that never interested me the way this did. But at sixteen to get on a big heavy sidecar, that took some determination. It was an obsession with me – it was more than an interest, more than a hobby – a proper obsession, I would call it. In spite of this, I still didn't know what I was doing, and at that point nobody would tell me. My mum still had to sign my racing licence off, and she had to give her consent to me racing until I was eighteen. That must have been difficult for her. It took a long time as well before other riders would accept me; to me it seemed to take a while anyway. I do think there was a reluctance there from those guys towards helping me. Anyone who was around my dad, the older established riders, I think they shied off, and didn't want to encourage me. That's my assumption anyway, but I think that's a fair thing to assume. I don't really blame them, to be honest – after all, it was only three years earlier that my dad had lost his life. But I was driven, and I wanted to do it. When I started to go alright, and I was safe, other people showed an interest then in helping. Billy Quayle was the biggest helper I had, at that time. It then went on to be Eric Bregazzi, who was the biggest help I've ever had.

It was only the year after my father and George had been killed that Howard Oates had started racing at Jurby airfield. I was stood on the sidelines watching, because I was still too young, but from that point on I felt that I would rather be driving than be a passenger. It was absolutely nothing to do with my dad being killed as a passenger, I can say that with certainty. The funny thing is, though, that it was almost expected of both Howard and myself that we would go into racing. In an odd sort of way it was considered an inevitability that it would happen, that Howard and I would end up competing in sidecars. How it was going to happen, Christ knows, because neither of us had any money. But it did happen, and by the time I started, Howard already had a couple of years under his belt, so instead of being passenger and driver we were racing against each other! I seem to remember that in those early days there was a bit of rivalry between us, which was a bit sad in a way really because it would have been nice for us to have raced together. I even think he would have made a bloody good passenger, because he had the right build for it. Howard saw himself as a driver, though, which was a natural progression, given that his dad had been successful at that.

But that bike I got in Liverpool was the biggest pile of shit you've ever seen; that was because I didn't know what I was buying, other than it had three wheels and a shiny fairing on it. The frame was a dog, and the thing as a whole was pretty battered. Two weeks after I had left school, and I'd got my first couple of wage packets (I was on fifteen quid a week then or something like that) I went straight round to the Isle of Man Bank and borrowed another £350 to buy a road bike. It was a GT750 Suzuki. I broke it, I took the engine out, and I fitted it into the frame of the outfit which I had just bought. When I say I didn't get a lot of help in those early days, I need to qualify that a bit because Ernie Leece also let me keep the sidecar in his old garage down on the quayside in Peel. He also helped with all the engine brackets, and we nailed the thing together, basically. I remember I had my first ride on that sidecar with my old schoolfriend, Paul Craine. We always called him 'Sid' because he was a punk rocker. (I think he might have been the Isle of Man's only punk rocker at that time, and he adopted the name 'Sid Vicious'!) So Sid and myself had our first ride on a sidecar up at Andreas airfield, an old run-down disused RAF airbase with grass sods growing up through the tarmac. I was not long gone sixteen at that time. Sid's dad had towed us down there in his old Escort van, and we were trying to make headway going round in circles, making a pretty poor effort of it, I seem to remember. While we were there this guy turned up, a bit of a bike supporter who I think went drinking with Sid's dad, and I don't think he thought we would come to much at all. In fact I think most people thought we wouldn't come to much; it may not have looked like we would, in all fairness, with this heap of a sidecar and two lads on it who really did not know what they were doing.

But during the course of that year Sid and I got our act together a bit, and then went out to our first ever race meeting. It was at Jurby airfield, in April 1980, and we were on that outfit that I had bought in Liverpool. It was an Isle of Man Centre championship round. Not only did we finish that race, we got third place in our first event, which is something I will never forget! We got a little wooden trophy, which I've still got. It's one of my proudest possessions. The machine, though, was a real cobbled-together thing; it had Mini wheels on it, and I only did about three races on it in total before it fell by the wayside. I couldn't *afford* to race, that was the truth of it, but the following year I got another bank loan, I think it was £1,000 this time. I got on the boat again and went and bought a better bike – on this occasion it was a Windle outfit. It was an extremely cheap bike for what it was, a real good bike, and at seventeen years old as I was then I got some really good results on that thing. I started going really well. At that time I was still doing Jurby airfield and the odd trip to England. I did Cadwell Park, and a couple of races at Flookburgh, which is up in Cumbria. It's not used any more that circuit, but that is where I won my first ever race – I had a few crashes there too! In those days you first had to get your National Licence, so you had to do twenty race meetings and get a signature for each just to get that piece of paper. Once you'd got it, you had to gain I think it was twenty points at National level, in order to get a one-event International Licence which would allow you to do the TT. That was a real difficult thing to do: you got six points for a win, five for a second place, and so on down like that. I didn't get my National Licence for two, nearly three years, and then when I did get it I was actually going quick enough to get some good results at National level.

Later, in 1982 when I was eighteen years old, I wanted to go to Flookburgh racing with Sid again. I'd been given this old Transit van; it had bald tyres, a knackered propshaft, and the floor was rusted out, you could actually see the road through it. I had no driving licence, and neither did Sid. We had no insurance, and no tax. We had taken the tax disc out of Sid's motorbike and put that in the windscreen, but we had no one else to take us to Flookburgh to go racing and get our licence, so we had no choice but to go in the van! We sat at the docks in Douglas waiting to board the boat, and both of us were shitting ourselves thinking, 'If the cops come now we've had it!' But we got on OK and off the other side, and we were on our way to Flookburgh when Sid turned to me and said, 'Listen, we're going to have to be careful at this event because if I take any more time off work they're going to bloody sack me, so we don't need to crash or anything like that ...!' Well, what happened? We won our heat, then went out in the final and we turned the bike over and crashed it! We both ended up in some hospital on the coast in Cumbria. There was me with a neck brace and chipped vertebrae, and Sid with his shoulder all battered, having to go back to his work on a lathe in some factory!

Around that time I was constantly at the bank, every year I went back for more money. In 1982, at just eighteen years old, I went and borrowed £2,000 in order to buy a better bike. I didn't need any security, I just went and told them I needed to buy a new bike, and it was 'there you go'! But I was ducking and diving as well, wheeling and dealing on cars, bodging things up to make ends meet. My work by this time had changed. I had started at Empire Garage because that was where my dad had worked, but I actually didn't like it, didn't like it at all. I think it was a bit too disciplined for me, because I was a bit rebellious. Also, I couldn't handle the fact there were nine mechanics there and three apprentices, and I was the youngest. Because of this I'd arrive at work, and not long after that, at half past nine, I'd have to start taking down the orders of who was eating what at ten o'clock in the morning. So then I'd get a hard time off the foreman for taking half an hour to take nine orders and run down town, get all these pies and shite like that, and come back with them all. But before all that I had to light the bloody oil-fired burner when I first got to work in the morning, then clear up after them all, and I just thought, 'I'm spending half the day clearing up shite after these fat bastard mechanics, who are as ignorant as fuck, treat you like shit, and thank you for nothing.' So I went to the foreman one day and said, 'When am I actually going to get to hold a spanner in this job, because I've been six months here and all I'm doing is cleaning up everybody's shit?' That was quite literally true, because the day they told me I had to go and clean the toilet, and it was like the toilet from hell, I just refused. They threatened to dunk me in the paraffin drum, and all this shit that you usually get when you're an apprentice, and I told them, 'You know what, you can all go to fucking hell!' I walked down to the main boss Dicky Craine's office and said, 'This ain't for me – you're employing a bunch of pricks, I'm off to get a different job.'

I walked out, I just left, and I got the bus from Peel to Ramsey, and went straight to another garage where I knew things were a bit more relaxed when it came to the pecking order. I asked in there, 'Would you give me a job?' John Faloon ran that garage, I'm friends with that guy to this day, and he said, 'I'll give you a job, you'll be on £19.50 a week, get here by nine on Monday morning. If you're not here by nine, don't make any excuses, just don't turn up.' And so I was there at half past eight, ready and raring to go. The first job I was given was to take the engine out of a Vauxhall Viva, and that was like a dream come true for me. From that point on, I got on great with those guys at that place. The garage closed eventually, and they then went into car bodywork. They'd seen me working on a sidecar fairing, spray-painting it, sign-writing on it (because I'd picked up brush sign-writing as well) and they asked if I wanted to work with them. I'd picked up enough mechanics to get by (though I hadn't done a full apprenticeship) and they taught me the bodywork side of things, which I still love. I still love painting, which I learned with them.

The guy I worked with at that time, Graham Cannell, was a fantastic motorcycle rider. He was without question the best raw talent that has ever come out of the Isle of Man, but he didn't even know it himself. Graham won the 1981 Lightweight Manx Grand Prix. He was so talented it was unbelievable. He was only about three or four years older than me, but I really looked up to him, I thought the sun shone out of his ass! I quite often went away with him to race meetings. He had pretty good sponsorship because he was really talented, he could win at National level, he could win at International level, and he had second places at the TT when he should really have won those races. Graham was a huge influence on me; when he raced he had a proper champion's aggression about him and a proper champion's attitude. As far as he was concerned he was unbeatable, he was a winner. He won the European Pro-Am Championship, he could outfox Niall Mackenzie, Alan Carter, Donnie McLeod and others. The best riders of the day, he could outfox them all. But he was extremely underrated, and not at all recognized. I think that was really down to his motivation, because he could not give a shit, he really couldn't. It was a shame that, because if he'd been a bit more interested he'd have gone to the highest level, without question. But I loved going away with Graham, and his sponsor actually paid me to go with him to keep the bikes nice and clean, and run round after him and that sort of thing, which I loved. I absolutely loved it.

During that time, it was the 1982 TT, Graham had Dale Singleton,[4] who was the Daytona 200 winner of that year, come over to him and ask if he could garage with him. So Graham opened his garage up to him, and said, 'Yeah, feel free.' Dale Singleton was a top six Grand Prix runner, in 500cc Grands Prix against Kenny Roberts, Barry Sheene and all those at that time, and he actually asked me if I would jack my job in with Graham and come and work for him, and do all the European circuit meetings. But I turned it down, because I was so obsessed with my own dream of being a sidecar winner, and I knew that if I went with him, I might like it more than I realized. So, for the fear of liking what I was being offered, I turned that offer down. To be honest, I don't have any regrets at all. It was a crossroads in my life, and if I had accepted the offer it would have taken me into a completely different world, and my life would have been totally different now. This guy, Dale Singleton, he was a fantastic bloke, really great, but he came to the TT, and maybe he did use it a bit, because he did get a huge start money cheque (figures like ten grand were being batted around at the time, in 1982) and he didn't put his best efforts in. He was a fabulous rider and he went straight from the TT, where he did dismally, to finish in the top six in the Czech Grand Prix! But he had full factory Yamaha backing, and my life would have been a different story if I'd gone there. The fact is I was scared, scared that I'd like it, and that I would forget my own dream of being a world champion, so that's why I didn't go. However, I did stay working with my mate Graham Cannell, working under him at the garage. He was too lazy even to run his own bikes in down at Jurby airfield (which was open to any member of the public back then), so he'd say to me, 'Dave, just take the van down to bloody Jurby and run my bikes in for me!' There I'd be, riding these pukka Grand Prix 250 Hondas or Yamahas or whatever. I'd be running in these things, going up and down, thinking I was the next best thing to Kenny Roberts. It was fantastic! They were really good times and I was heavily influenced by Graham's attitude, I think, because he was so good. Of course, I still had the memory of George O'Dell, who was my boyhood hero, running round in my head as well.

Around this time I also got married for the first time. The truth of the matter was that I was still very young – looking back I was too young – and if I'm honest the main reason I got married so early in life was in order to get away from my situation at home where I was still very unhappy. Inevitably, it seems now, the marriage was doomed to fail, and it did. The only positive thing which came out of that relationship was my daughter Cheryl, who was born in 1984 and of whom I am tremendously proud. She isn't interested in the TT or sidecars, though, and any conversation about motorbikes is a non-starter with her!

The first year that I took on the TT was 1985, but it was a load of bollocks. I should never have done it, but I thought I was capable of winning it – maybe not at that point, but capable one day of winning it – and I was that hell-bent on doing it that I figured, the earlier I get in the better. I didn't take advice too well, which I should have done; but I was in my early twenties, and I would have done just about anything to get into the TT. So again I went to the bank, and with the money I borrowed I bought another outfit – this time it was a 750cc Yamaha. On paper it was a good bike, but when I got it out on the track it was a bad bike. It blew up in both sidecar TT races and I didn't complete a single lap! I had to beg to get into the event in the first place, I'd got my entry refused at first by the organizers, and after hammering on the door day in and day out, the day before practice started they eventually gave in and gave me a ride. I'd been refused on the grounds of not enough experience, basically. In spite of the points I'd gained racing in England and at Jurby, they still felt I wasn't up to the standard needed for the TT, but I was given the chance anyway. Doug Barnfield, who was the Auto-Cycle Union (ACU) chairman at the time, he OK'd it, and I started at number 93, last away. Although I was quite fast (I was probably only 10 miles an hour off the lap record, which was pretty good at that time), that first TT fucked me up financially so badly that it looked like that was me finished racing for good. Jesus, I'd borrowed three grand to get into the thing, which in 1985 was a hell of a lot of money, and now the bike was totally wrecked.

But then I had some unexpected help come my way from Eric Bregazzi. He'd helped me out previously, in a smaller way, but now he got me an engine for the Southern 100.[5] We broke down in our heat, which was a bummer, because we were going really well, but we won the consolation race dead easily, so it was a good win, at a national

event. After that I had Eric's support for a number of years, right up
to the mid-1990s. Eric is an electrician, from Union Mills on the Isle
of Man. He started racing around the same time as my dad, and they
were friends; it wasn't just advice and supplies which he gave to me,
Eric and his father Dick Bregazzi also helped me out financially in a
big way. I wasn't going to be racing again after that first TT but then
Eric and his dad came along. The following year they offered me their
bike, which was a really good one, a top-class machine in fact. Eric
retired from racing himself, and I started on his bike, with his gear,
and it was from then on that I really started doing things. We won the
Southern 100, we won some good national races in England, and we
were lying in the top three at the 1986 TT, in the second race, when
we broke down on the last lap. We broke down on the last lap of the
first race while holding sixth place as well, so we'd arrived, we were
there, and everybody knew it.

The people to beat back then were Mick Boddice,[6] Lowry Burton,
and Nigel Rollason. There was a whole string of really class acts at the
TT then. It was not that long after the death of Jock Taylor,[7] Sidecar
World Champion, who had the TT lap record at the time. I remember
Dick Greasley and Steve Abbott (who was a World Championship
contender), they were all there, World Championship and British
Championship contenders, and there was me mixing it amongst
them, which felt really good. There was also a lot of camaraderie at
the TT in those days, everyone would help you out – racing back then
was a lot different. We were all on the same engines, which was a help.
It was the best engine you could have, and we were all able to get that
engine. It was the readily available TZ750 Yamaha, and if we did a
crank, we could go to the next van and they'd have a crank, or if not
then to one further down the paddock. Somebody would have a
crankshaft to help you out. You could rebuild these engines yourself;
they weren't specialist build, they were pretty simple engines to work
with, as they were two-strokes. Cylinders, pistons, you name it,
cylinder heads, you could get them from anybody, beg borrow or

whatever, you'd get through. I was also lucky at this time, as I got involved with some other good people who really helped me out. Billy Boyd, who was running the Ginger Hall Hotel at the time, him and the guys who used to go in there drinking regularly and their wives, they would support us. It was a great bunch of people. Every Sunday, for instance, they'd go in there and support the raffles towards us, and Billy would raise a bit of money towards boat fares and things like that to get off the Island. We had probably six or eight people who were really good helpers at the time. I couldn't have carried on racing without them, they were just brilliant people.

In 1985 my old school buddy Sid (Paul Craine) retired from racing, and I got a guy called Paul Kneale on as passenger. Paul lived on the Sulby Straight, and at that time he was racing with Billy Boyd from the Ginger Hall Hotel. In March 1986 I bumped into them at Jurby airfield. Paul was driving a sidecar at that time and Billy was his passenger, but he decided that he didn't want to go out after all. He asked me if I would go on the side with Paul instead, because I wasn't racing that day. I said, 'I'm not going on the side of any sidecar, but I'll drive it if you want?' So we changed the entry details, because you could sign up on the day back then, and Paul passengered while I drove. After that, I asked him if he wanted to do the TT with me that year. He was probably in his mid to late thirties at that point, which is pretty late on for a sidecar passenger. It was a shame really because he was coming to the end of his racing career and I was just starting mine. Being a passenger, you need to be a bit more athletic, and I think he was struggling with his fitness a little bit, so in the end he went back to being a sidecar driver. But we had some great rides, he was with me when I won the 1986 Southern 100, and in 1987 we were actually billed as the only pair who could really give Mick Boddice a run for his money in the TT. It was headlined in the *MotorCycle News*: 'Can Molyneux beat Boddice?', and I was just blown away by that, because at that point I'd hardly even begun to make a mark at the TT, in fact I hadn't even finished a race. We went into it that year,

1987, and we were really quick in practice, in fact we led a couple of sessions on the leader board. I also remember one particular incident, which occurred during that practice week: I was about to go out one evening when I was approached by a steward and asked to go up to race control. I went with him and was taken to a small room where three stewards and a policeman were waiting. I asked what was going on and was told it was best if I only answered the questions that were being put to me. I answered with an expletive and was told by the cop that if there was any more of that kind of language, I would be taken to another room and dealt with very differently. It was just like being a naughty boy back at school!

It turned out that this was all connected with an incident the evening before. The previous night there had been a big crash in practice out beyond Crosby Hill at what used to be the Wagon and Horses pub. As it happened, I'd had a misfire coming into Crosby on that lap, so I had pulled into Crosby Wholesalers, and Paul and I set about changing the spark plug. As we set off again, we saw the yellow flags out well before we reached the scene. Well, that looked like a real car crash but we toured right through it, and I had my hand in the air to acknowledge the flags of the marshals. When we came round again, the scene had been cleared, but now these stewards at the Grandstand were telling me that I had been reported by a marshal for firstly riding at a reckless speed through the scene of an incident, and secondly not acknowledging the signals of the marshals. Well, I was bloody fuming about this, I really was. I really don't take it well if people accuse me of something that I haven't done and back in those days I was seriously headstrong anyway.

I told these stewards about the misfire, and the fact that I had about a dozen witnesses in the Crosby pub who saw me acknowledging the marshals. I was still seething when I went out to practise that night and as a result I rode like an arsehole, as I had all this stuff still going around in my head. I told Eric about it when I got back in. He went and complained about the way I'd been treated – he was a bit of a father figure to me was Eric – and he was as annoyed as I was about the way I'd been dragged away just as I was about to go out, still wearing my gloves and helmet. Anyway, it transpired that the marshal had reported a blue and white bike which turned out to be number 81. We were blue and white and number 18, so he'd got confused had this guy. We got an apology in the end from the Clerk of the Course over that incident.

Well, the first race came, and the bloody gear lever came adrift on the mountain, so we stopped up there, put the gear lever back on, and got going again. We were lying second at that point behind Boddice, but we dropped back to nineteenth place on that second lap, because of the stop. Then we pitted as well to make a better repair, got going again and ended up clawing our way back up to tenth, so that was our first result. We went out in the second race and on the first lap we were leading it by 11 seconds at Ballaugh, which was some lead, but the rear wheel broke going up the Mountain Mile. Well, that was it, game over for us. So that was our third TT, but you could hardly really class it as our third one, because we had so few laps under our belts from our previous outings at the event. We didn't do any laps in our first TT, in the second TT we probably did something like four laps of practice, and four laps of racing (two in each race) and then in 1987 we probably did something like six laps of practice and three laps in the first race, so we had no experience really, yet here we were leading a bloody TT, and at my age as well, I was only about twenty-two or twenty-three.

Looking back on those days I think I was pretty crazy. I've always had a reputation as quite arrogant and I probably come over as that sometimes, but then some people deal with their nerves and their focus in a different way from other people; some people will be laughing and joking, some people will be deadly serious. You've only got to look at the likes of Carl Fogarty[8] and people like that. You've got Valentino Rossi, the joker of the pack, and then you've got Jorge Lorenzo with a face like thunder. They go out and do the same job; it's just how people are perceived and I think it's a bit unfair really. But I know I had an awful lot of self-belief back then. I remember one guy in a local pub saying to me, just before the 1986 Southern 100, 'So how d'you think you'll do in the Southern 100, Dave?' and I just said, 'I'll win it.' This guy was a bit taken aback and came back at me, 'You fucking cocky twat!!' I answered him quite calmly, 'Well, ... I will. I'll win this event.' I was right. I won my heat and I won the final. The thing was, I was that pumped up with self-belief that I thought, 'I've got the gear, I've got the tackle and I *can* do this,' and I did. I know it sounds cocky and arrogant but I was that driven, I was obsessed with it, this was what I wanted to do. My ambitions were huge – World Champion, that's where I wanted to be, which I never did achieve, but I tried – in my own mind I was going all the way. I wasn't just going to stop, I wasn't going to be contented just by winning the TT, or the Southern 100, or winning a few races in England which I was doing anyway; my ambition was to go all the way.

These days I've got a bit more of a sense of self-preservation when I'm racing, but back in those days, in my twenties, I took it right to the edge. I don't think other riders thought of me as reckless, but I remember a couple of people saying to me, 'Bloody hell, Dave, cool it a bit, you're using too much of the track.' What they didn't realize was that was my style, I still use that style today. They were confusing the fact that I was 3 inches from the kerb with the idea that it was too close, too dangerous or on the edge. But my race craft that I learned showed me that using tight lines slowed you down. Using big, wide lines speeded you up, so when I got close to a kerb it was because I calculated it. I didn't do it because I'd made a mistake; I did hit kerbs occasionally, because I made a mistake, but a lot of those old-style riders would give themselves 12 inches of space whereas I would give myself 3 inches. You could say the same thing about Joey Dunlop.[9] In his early years, people thought he was ragged, they thought he was rough, but that was his appearance, it wasn't his riding style. He did take it to the edge of the track, but he did it for thirty years, and as time moved on they realized that he was doing that on purpose; you could put a coin on that part of the track and he'd cross it every time, that's what he was doing, and people say that about me now. Yes, I made mistakes, racing mistakes, when I was younger but I never went out not caring about whether I hurt my passenger, the people sitting watching on the hedge, or myself, and I very rarely did.

Regarding passengers, I always went for who I considered to be the best. I wasn't shy of asking someone who was already riding with somebody else. It was frowned upon a bit, was that. But then if you want to be the best, you've got to have the best people around you, and that means the whole team, the whole set-up. I felt that if that person thought I was the best chance of winning, I would make them an offer. I always thought that people thought the same way as me – but often they didn't! So when I went to this person I would be full of confidence that they thought I was going to be the next best thing since sliced bread, and I was offering them a chance to be alongside that, because I thought they could be. That was my way of thinking – it might have been the wrong way – but I went in there bold as brass, and just said, 'Fancy riding with me next year, because I can take this right to the top; do you want to be with it, or not?' Some of them said yes, and some of them said no. But I would ask anybody really.

It was in 1989 that we won our first TT. Colin Hardman[10] was my passenger now. He and I had been to Cadwell Park in Lincolnshire, two weeks before the TT that year, and had a huge crash, a massive crash. I'd had several other crashes prior to that one, but nothing as heavy as this, it was a real scary one. We completely wrote off our short circuit bike and both of us spent the night in Louth Infirmary with concussion, bashed to buggery, cuts, bruises, everything but broken bones really. We were only at Cadwell Park testing, we hadn't ridden that year, and that was our first event, we were just shaking the machine down. But we picked up a rear wheel puncture on the back straight, we went round the right-handers, and it was wheel-spinning quite a bit. I thought, 'This is weird.' I flicked it into the left-hander at the top of the hill and the ass of the bike met the front and over it went. It was a steep downhill section from the gooseneck, and we went about 300 yards end over end. I actually thought that Colin was a lot more seriously hurt than he was. He was unconscious for ten minutes. I was out cold for two or three minutes, until they pulled me round. Christ, I had a shock when I saw Colin, I thought he was worse than he actually was. But we got over that, and we went home.

We next went out at Jurby road circuit on the Saturday morning before the TT started. We won that race but we were well battered, we were well and truly knocked about. On Monday morning we went out to practise for the TT for the first time. Our TT bike was fabulous, just *brilliant*; we'd worked hard on it over the winter, Eric Bregazzi and myself. The bike had a Trevor Ireson chassis, which Eric and his dad had bought for us in 1988. That was arguably the best chassis to have at the TT at that time, and we had mutually agreed to go with the Ireson, but I have to say I never liked it. I never liked the style of the fairing and bodywork, even though Trevor had spent long hours at some university in a wind tunnel designing it and testing it. It had been a huge task for him, but somehow when you were on the bike you always felt that you were perched on top of it, not in it. You were exposed to the wind, so you ended up putting Perspex bubbles on the front of the bike to try to give yourself some protection from the buffeting. I began to suspect it had been designed with no rider or passenger on it. It was like a projectile, with no consideration given to the rider, and as soon as you put that person on it, he was getting covered in shit, flies, oil, anything really from the elements. It felt like you were perched on the back of a rocket, going through the air! So I was never happy with the bodywork, and during that winter I persuaded Eric to let me have a go at creating this bullet-shaped fairing, which to my mind was more streamlined. We went into the 1989 TT with it, and Trevor Ireson was there. He saw it and he said to us, 'You've fucked that bike right up by putting that bodywork on;

you've made it worse, not better!' But I already had an understanding of how these things worked and I knew it did feel better.

By the middle of practice week we were quickest, and then we just got pipped towards the end of the week by Mick Boddice. Strangely, the crash at Cadwell Park hadn't shaken us up mentally, we were just so keen to get out there, after all the work we'd done over the winter. But then at the end of practice week, on the Friday morning, my brother Graham and I were going up to work on the bike at Union Mills, at Eric Bregazzi's house, and we had Manx Radio on. We'd not taken part in morning practice that day, and the shocking news came over that Phil Hogg had been killed. Phil was a local rider, really talented, and he was going places. He was a fearless kid, and he'd lost it at Glen Vine, and was killed. The whole Island was shaken up by it. He was a red-hot talent and people had high hopes for him being successful, in a similar way to Conor Cummins, really, at the TT today. So there we were, working in the garage, my brother knew Phil Hogg quite well. I knew him but not well, but my brother was gutted. We were working on the bike, in readiness for our first race, and Rob Brew called into the garage to see us, the guy who had knocked me over when I was a kid. Rob had won the Manx Grand Prix himself in his younger days, and was a great supporter of racing, but he called into the garage, where it was all pretty sombre, and I can't remember his exact words but it was something like, 'Well, I'll not hang around, boys, but remember we're all depending on you now.' It just wasn't what we wanted to hear. It just added to the pressure, and I don't mind admitting, I felt like cracking. It was a very black time, we'd just lost one of the best, and we'd nearly written ourselves off a couple of weeks before. Added to all this, during practice week – I think it was on the Tuesday night when we were quickest – we were going through Gorse Lea just after the Hawthorn, and there were flags out all over the place. Franco Martinel and his passenger had just had a big accident there, and the passenger Marco Fattorelli got killed. I didn't know that at the time but I knew it was a bloody big crash. Then a few miles down the road, at the top of Barregarrow, John Mulcahy crashed and he was killed. It was pretty shocking, in fact it was mind-blowing, but I just kept going and we ended up actually being quickest that night. It was a strange feeling as I came into the paddock. The helicopter had just landed, and there were people crying, his family I guess, that was the worst thing.

So really it was a very bad time. Nevertheless, seeing people get killed or hearing about it never really made me think, 'I'm not going to go out and do this any more.' I always felt, 'I've got to do this, and I've got to do it the best that I can.' If you feel that it's dangerous, then you have to deal with it at the time. I've gone through serious accidents, and I've slowed it right up for a good few miles afterwards, I've stopped racing and I'm just touring almost, thinking, 'What is going on here?' but I never wanted to give up racing. It's an unfortunate side of it, but I think you do get used to it, and *maybe* my dad losing his life all those years ago had an effect on me. I don't know, perhaps I can handle it differently from some other people.

Well, we went into the first race, and we'd had constant reliability problems prior to that year, for years before in fact, but that year we cracked it, Eric and his father and myself. I never would have won that first TT without their support, but in 1989 with their help, and with the help of a few others, we put together a really decent package; we got that bike competitive. So we went into that first race pretty confident, both in ourselves and our ability, and also in the bike itself. In fact it was clear by that stage that it was really a very good bike. It was a strange race, because we got set off on the wrong start time. There was somebody in front of us who missed his start position, and that set the grid off in the wrong sequence. So I got to the end of the race, and I thought we'd finished second, losing out by a couple of seconds. But I was pretty happy with that because it was a hard race, and the bike didn't run exceptionally well; it could have run better. Two-strokes are very fickle, and on that particular day it could have run a lot better. When you get to the bottom of Bray Hill, you usually know if the bike is going any good, and on this occasion it just didn't feel that great; but we just accepted that, it was our fault because we'd set it up. But we got to the Park Fermé afterwards well happy at the thought we'd finished second, and then somebody, I think it was Geoff Cannell, the roaming commentator, came and said, 'Something's wrong here, Dave has won it, he ain't second.' There was a lot of confusion, but then it was announced over the tannoy that we'd actually won the race on corrected time, because there had been this cock-up on the start line. So it was official that we'd actually won the race! It was a rollercoaster of emotions for me. Deep down I was a little disappointed in the fact that the bike had not gone as well as it had done in practice, and with such a small margin of losing out, I thought, you know, if it had been right we could have walked that race, but then at the same time I figured, 'What the hell, we're second, it's my first podium position ever, so that'll do for today. We'll have better luck next time.' And the next thing I know, I've won it! Luckily this was all sorted out in the Park Fermé, before we went up onto the rostrum, so we went up there as winners! We got the champagne, and the winners' laurels on our first time up there. But my memories of that first win are hazy. It's something I remember very little of. People might find that a little bit strange, I suppose, and also the fact that when I look back on it, I think it was quite hard to enjoy that moment. Although there's no denying that the winning of the TT is a great thing, and the enormity of it all is fabulous – it's a *big* thing, and it really keeps you up there on your toes – it's also always very hectic at the end of a race. Everybody's talking to you, and everything seems to happen too fast. As soon as you get off that bike, everything seems to happen bang bang bang, one thing after another. Scrutineers want to see your bike, and if you haven't got a mechanic looking after your outfit they're expecting you there to assist them, and you are herded through a bit like cattle. It isn't as glamorous as it might look to those on the outside; in fact sometimes it's bloody shite to put it bluntly! It's not comfortable, for want of a better word; before you know it, it's all over and done, and you're just back sitting in your van thinking, 'Wow, that all just blew over. Where did it all go, the last hour and a half?'

The funny thing was, after we had won that first TT I had a few other competitors turn to me and actually say that I had an unfair advantage because of the bodywork I had created! I just thought, 'Where's the common sense behind that?' The bike's original fairing had been designed in a wind tunnel, but we'd knocked this bodywork up in a shed, and the truth is it *was* better. It handled better, and steered better and we went faster than we'd ever gone before. People can make sidecar racing far too technical, bringing in stuff from universities, Formula One racing cars or whatever. But these people aren't riders, nine times out of ten, and I believe that you've got to be riding these things in order to be able to bring them on. You've got to feel what's going on. That same year, 1989, we ran with Lectron carburettors on. They were a thing of the past, it's true, but we thought we'd try them, and the bike was fantastic with them on, a completely different machine. Dennis Trollope was helping us out a little bit at the time, with cheap oil, chains, that kind of thing, and he took a glance at the bike and said, 'What the hell are you doing with Lectron carbs on? You're not going to win any TTs with those things on!' My answer to that was, 'Well, Jock Taylor won with Lectron carbs, and no one has gone as fast as him yet!' That was the truth of it, and the ironic thing was that Dennis Trollope was Jock Taylor's sponsor at that time when he set the lap record at the TT. We stuck with it, and won our first TT with those things on! It was a funny thing how all of these people with all this knowledge were coming forward to condemn us, but we achieved that win in spite of what they were saying. We really used our heads that year, did Eric and myself. We stopped following people for the first time and started thinking for ourselves. We stepped back a stage and thought, 'This idea was working ten years ago, people left it behind, yet things haven't gone any faster in those ten years.' We re-examined what had happened in those years and where things had gone wrong. Eric and I put a lot of homework into all areas of that bike. Yes, we did use old ideas, but we also used fresh ideas as well, and as a combination it really came together for us.

Well, we'd won the first race that year, and then we were third in the second race. With the bike we had under us it could have been an even better result, but in that second trip out we got into a real dog-fight with two other riders. After we'd set off I'd caught them both up on the road; it was number 4, number 6 and I was number 7. We'd passed the number 5 bike well on, all of us, and now number 6, which was Dave Hallam, had caught up number 4, which was Geoff Rushbrook. I then caught up the two of them, and I passed Dave Hallam, the number 6 bike, and got between them. But it was like a sandwich through the whole race, it was bloody horrendous. Rushbrook was all over the place, he wasn't very good on the track, he was never on the same line twice, and I didn't find he was very gentlemanly when it came to passing; I attempted to pass him on a number of occasions where I definitely had the line and he chopped me up. He put me up the kerb at Lambfell on the second lap, and I just thought, 'Fuck this … I'm not here to die, I'm here to race. You don't want to race, you just want to make it into a game of stock cars and I'm not here for that.' So I just rode round biding my time and being patient. I was lying in second place while I was in that dice, while Mick Boddice was creeping away. There was nothing I could do about this, short of risking hurting myself and Colin, and I chose not to do that. So in the last lap, on the run across the mountain, we were stuck in this dice and I ended up losing second place. We finished third. I remember being pretty pissed off about that afterwards, not because of the result, but because it just wasn't the way I like to do things, and I still don't today. I've actually stopped riding at some events, because of the way certain other people ride when racing at them.

Chapter 2

In It To Win It

In 1989 we had won our first TT, the goal which I and the people helping and supporting me had been working towards for almost a decade. Yet every penny we had won in prize money at that TT was swallowed up by the enormous cost of racing there. We had lots of people chipping in at the time, but even so we'd come out of the TT in debt, which we would have to sort out, one way or another. The prize money never cleared anything like what we'd spent getting into the thing in the first place. Even so, that didn't dent my enthusiasm by any means. However, the same couldn't be said for Colin, sadly. This event went by, and he just kind of lost interest. It was like he'd won the TT ... and that was it. So I got Alan Langton back on, who'd ridden with me before Colin. In the 1990 season, the TT changed massively for sidecars, with the event going to Formula Two class. That change was prompted by the generally poor state of sidecars at that time. Outfits were being built for 500cc and 750cc two-stroke engines, which were tiny engines. They were quite lightweight, and intended for Grand Prix use, really. People were then buying these bikes second-hand, and adapting them to fit a cost-effective engine to go TT racing with. This would usually be a 1,000cc Suzuki, Kawasaki or Honda, big four-strokes which were nearly double the weight of the engine that the chassis was originally designed to carry. So accidents were happening because of this; frames were breaking, and people were losing their lives because the general state of the bikes was dreadful. In the end the ACU had to do something. The machines at the TT weren't getting any faster, they were just getting more dangerous. So they thought, if they changed the rules, people would have to build new bikes, and build them suited to the engines they were actually going to use. The specification for TT sidecars was reduced from 1,000cc down to Formula Two spec, which was 350cc. You could also ride a 600cc four-stroke in Formula Two as you can today, but those engines were so old-fashioned and heavy in those days that they just weren't competitive against a 350cc two-stroke Yamaha. So that was what we opted for.

I was dead against that change, at the time. To me it bordered on the ridiculous to change from a 1,000cc limit to a 350cc limit. Then they also threw in the four-stroke 600cc class, and it wasn't even filtered into the event, they just dumped it on the TT's doorstep. Today it's a great class, and, looking back, they made the correct decision to bring that in. But they got that right by sheer luck, not by judgement, because it took a long time for the 600cc engines to *develop* into a great racing class. Back in 1990, 600cc four-strokes were not even a great solo class. It's fair to say that, because not all the manufacturers even produced a decent engine for racing at that size back then. I think they brought that class in to keep people like me pacified; people who didn't like the fact that all their hard work and all the sponsorship they had raised – tens of thousands of pounds' worth to finance these 750cc two-stroke Yamahas that we were running – had just been dumped down the bloody drain. Other people were running 1,000cc Suzukis or Kawasakis or whatever, and just like ours these bikes became obsolete in terms of the TT literally overnight. They were just scrap. You had a TT-winning bike one day, and then the next you had a bike that didn't suit the TT or anywhere else for that matter. As it happens, the ACU did have a history of doing this sort of thing at that time; they would chop classes, without any real forethought. I think so, anyway.

For myself and Eric, it was a lot of hard work down the pan as well, because we had spent two years developing our Trevor Ireson chassis into something really special. I'd just won a TT in 1989, but I could never use the machine I had ridden again, and to go into 1990 I had to make a choice. Nothing was proven in the 600cc four-stroke game, so we thought we had to go with the 350cc two-stroke in order to be competitive. But we'd never ridden this thing before. To adapt your riding style to this new machine, and still try to be competitive and try and win (which is what we were there for, after all) in that short space of time, was sheer lunacy. I think it needed maybe two years to filter this idea in, but we had just nine months to sort this out and we either did the TT or we didn't. So of course we had a brand-new bike bought for us. Our sponsor Frank Higley and his wife supplied a brand-new chassis; with Eric Bregazzi and his dad, and a few other helpers on the Island, we also got these 350cc Yamaha engines together. The bike was around half the weight of what we were used to riding, and we got it less than a week before the start of the TT, so we hadn't tested it or run it. I didn't adapt too well to it, but then I hadn't really been given much of a chance! The net result was that we had a massive crash in practice, at Laurel Bank; a huge crash in fact. That was entirely because I was so inexperienced on that new machine. I was twenty-five years old, I'd just won a TT and naturally I wanted to go out and defend what I'd won, but I was put on an alien machine to do it; it just wouldn't happen today. Nowadays you have to get a TT circuit licence, do a minimum of six events, go to club meetings and so on just to get a signature to ride in the TT, whereas back then they just chucked you out on a bike that could bloody kill you!

Sure enough, during our first session of practice the bike went into a violent slide; it broke away very fast in fifth gear. It flung Alan, my passenger, out, and then it dug in, pitched over and landed on top of me. We slid down the road upside down and hit the rock face at Laurel Bank. Being trapped under the bike was probably a good thing, because the machine took all of the impact, while I didn't make contact with the wall. Then the bike cartwheeled further down the road and I was just left lying at the foot of the rock face. I got up instantly, because we were first on the road and I didn't want to get hit by a following machine. I ran across the road to the hedge and sat down with all the breath taken out of me. Keith Trubshaw, one of the Travelling Marshals, came running up the road. Alan was still lying in the road about a hundred yards further back, on the right-hand bend as you come into Laurel Bank One. I was really scared about him, as he was lying unmoving across the white line in the road. The other marshals ran up to Alan, while Keith Trubshaw came up to me, and said, 'Are you alright?' I told him that I didn't feel too good, so he unzipped my leathers at the front. Straight away we saw that my shoulder had got embedded in my ribcage. I'd sprung my sternum, broken some ribs down my left-hand side and broken my shoulder and collarbone. It was all just shoved in, and I had this huge lump on the front of my chest where everything had been compacted and pushed forward. I'm no medical expert but I knew right away it didn't look good. As I'd been trapped under the bike while it slid along I'd been cut to ribbons, and there was a lot of meat off me. They also thought I'd broken my foot; I knew something was wrong as soon as I stood up and ran with it. Keith unzipped my boot and took it off, and straight away my foot blew up like a balloon. It turned out not to be broken, but it had been bashed very hard. In fact both of my heels were very badly bruised where I came down on them. It looked at the time as if Alan's injuries were much worse, though. He was unconscious. There was a bit of an argument at the side of the road then between the medics and the marshals about who they would take to hospital. I can't really remember that clearly, but I think there was someone already in the emergency helicopter. Keith argued till he was blue in the face that I was in bad shock, and that I should go to hospital right away. They had already loaded Alan up by this time, and I must have been put in but they couldn't shut the door with us all in. I just remember being upside down as the helicopter banked and flew over Noble's Hospital, and absolutely shitting myself! I'd just been pelted down the road at 130 miles an hour, cut myself to ribbons and now here I was having my first ever ride in a helicopter, strapped to a stretcher and hanging upside down out of the door!

I got myself out of hospital after a couple of days; I signed myself out because I was that bloody depressed in there, one because I had crashed at the TT where I thought I would never crash – I really thought I would never crash at the TT – and I did, but secondly because I wrote the bike off, which was a big deal. We'd been well sponsored with the outfit, and a lot of time and effort had gone into it, and I wrote it off. I could see no way of getting back on track with that. It was a bloody depressing time; I was laid out there with people being shipped in with broken arms and legs, howling and screaming; I just thought, 'I'm out of here!' The next morning when the doctor came to me for the check-up, he said, 'The nurse tells me you want to leave.' I said yes. He then replied, 'Have you *seen* the state of your feet, never mind your top half?' I told him they felt a bit sore, that was all. He said, 'I'll tell you what, son, if you can walk the length of this bed within half an hour, I might let you go.' I had a box over my feet in the bed, so I thought, 'This can't be that bad.' I slung my feet out and put them down. Just the rush of blood to them from doing that had me in tears! I managed to get stood up on them after about fifteen minutes. I didn't walk, I just waited for the doc to come back. When he did reappear, I was leaning against the bed, and he said, 'Go on then, get walking.' I shuffled about half the length of the bed before he stopped me, saying, 'For God's sake sit down, you must be desperate to get out of here!' But he let me go all the same.

I was pretty knocked about, though, I really had got badly bust up in that crash, with a broken shoulder, ribs, sternum and all that stuff. Alan fractured his pelvis and got scarified. I had broken my left shoulder quite badly as it turned out. About three weeks later the doctors told me I needed an operation on it, and I asked how long I would need off work. They said I would need three months of rest to recuperate after the operation; I said, 'Well, I can't take three months off work; it's not even an option, so I'll leave it as it is.' I've left it like that to this day, it's never been repaired. By this time I'd got out of the car bodywork business. I was hod-carrying now on a building site, because they were paying *double* the wages at that time on building sites on the Isle of Man. That was a bit of a laugh, going back to work on a building site with a broken wing, and ribs and all, but I was carrying my bricks under my right arm instead of on a hod! They were a great bunch of lads I was working with then, though, Colin Kinnin, Billy Boyd and all that gang, they were just a real good bunch and they carried me along for a few months before they started kicking me up the arse and telling me to pull my weight again!

In spite of all that, I didn't lose my drive, I still thought I could get things back on track with my racing. I had big, big ambitions at that point. Once I'd won the TT I wanted to use that as a stepping stone to Grand Prix racing and I really thought – naively, I admit – that this TT win would be the making of me as a professional rider. I desperately wanted to go professional and ride in the World Championships, in fact I wasn't on my own in this, a number of people who supported me thought the same thing: we've got there now, and this thing is going to go sky's-the-limit. But it didn't! In fact it went the opposite way. It was a bad time generally to be looking for support. There were obvious dangers with motorcycle racing, a few local lads had got killed, and in 1989 the TT had had its worst casualties for many years. I think it frightened a few sponsors off. It was literally just bad timing. We just couldn't attract a big sponsor, and it was not for want of trying. Finances weren't that bad, we'd got over the mid-1980s recession, and there was money around; building was booming, but we couldn't for the life of us attract a backer to take us up to the next level of Grand Prix racing. We did try; my mates all clubbed together, and we bought this Grand Prix outfit for £6,000. Six of us all chucked a grand apiece in, and we bought this bike, and tried to break into it, but it just wasn't working.

Over the years we had a succession of shitty vans, one after another, mostly clapped out old Transits, but we upgraded to a Mercedes 609 van that year. Well, we thought we'd upgraded, but it was probably still ten years old at least. Even so, we painted it all up and made it look smart, and that Easter weekend of 1990 me and the half dozen or so mates who had chipped in decided to take this bike across to England and go racing, with us all crammed in the back of this van. We got off the boat from the Isle of Man at Heysham and our first port of call was to get race fuel. Well, we had to go to Blackpool Airport for that, because at the time that was the nearest place that you could get Avgas. So we went all the way down there, and then on the way back on the motorway just before we were going to join up with the M6 around Preston, the bloody big end went on this van. It was clanking like mad, so we were driving down the hard shoulder until we could turn off onto the A6 just outside Preston, and pulled into this fuel station. This was the day before Good Friday and we ended up staying there until Easter Sunday. We had the bottom of the engine pulled off behind this filling station. The guy who owned the petrol station loaned us a car, we went to a scrapyard and managed to find an engine that was the same. We pulled the big end shells out of it, and fitted them on the van round the back of the filling station. That was roadside recovery DIY style! We eventually got going late on the Sunday afternoon, heading for Oulton Park, where we raced on the Easter Monday.

But try as we might, we couldn't break into racing at that level, so I stepped back from it for a bit, and went really back to basics. I went back to club level almost, to just keep racing and try and keep the enthusiasm going between those of us who were involved. It was the only way we could afford to do it, because for whatever reason it just wasn't happening. In 1991 and 1992 we won Southern 100s, and we won lots of other races, like National League events. In 1991 we had third place at the TT, and in 1992 we again got a third place at the TT, all on pretty inferior engines. They were very slow and underpowered, only producing about 85 horsepower if the truth is known, but we got them up there in the top three with sheer hard work.

After the 1990 crash, Alan gave up sidecars and I got Karl Ellison on board. Karl is a couple of years older than me, and I had known him for a while. I had worked for his dad prior to our teaming up, and he used to call in to the garage and see me occasionally. Karl was really into bikes, and he was reasonably good on a solo. He had also ridden as a sidecar passenger before, around 1988, so he had a bit of experience there, and after the crash he asked me, 'What are you doing for a passenger?' I said, 'Well, I haven't got one at the minute, but when I get better after this accident I want to get riding again.' He said straight away, 'Well, I'll race with you!' and that turned out to be a bloody good move. That was a great team we put together. He was a really talented passenger; he was as skinny as a rake back then, but he was quite tall, so it was a good combination. Also, his attitude was very good. It helped me along because I was a bit down in the dumps then about not being able to afford to go Grand Prix racing and doing the things I wanted to, and he got me out of that, he sort of pulled it into line. He said, 'Well, let's just buy a cheap bike and go club racing and win some races.' We did and we had two bloody good years there on that one bike.

In 1992 for the first time I built my own bike, which I'm the first to admit wasn't a very good one. It had a slow engine and the chassis wasn't great, but I genuinely believed that I could build something myself which was more suited to my riding style. I'd ridden a Windle outfit, which I loved, but it was a difficult bike to ride. I liked it, but it was a very physical bike to handle. I rode a Colin Jacobs outfit, which was very heavy and cumbersome, and I rode a Trevor Ireson chassis which I won my first TT on, but I didn't like the bike, I never felt comfortable on it. I thought, 'I need to do something about this.' I'd taught myself welding in the car trade, and I thought, this is the only way I'm going to get a bike which suits my riding style, and is the way I want it to be, I've got to try this. That bike I built in 1992 was the cheapest of the cheap, the wheels were ten years old, the brakes were twenty years old, it was a real 'bitzer' bike. No one would sell me new components as I had no proven track record as a constructor, so I ended up buying an old bike to cannibalize for the parts I needed; I took no chances, though – I took all the vital parts like bearing seats down to the Ronaldsway Aircraft Company to get them tested for hairline cracks. Everything came back OK from them so I cobbled it all together, but the thing was, it worked, and that encouraged me to carry on.

Then in 1993 it all just came together, all that being patient and not so bloody headstrong started to pay off. The first bike I built that I put a real big effort into, and which needed money behind it, was the one I used in the 1993 TT. I put together what I really wanted to put together. It was my own design, which drew on elements of all the other bikes I had ever ridden, and there was a few grand chucked in the pot as well, from various local sponsors. It worked – it might have been a lucky design, I don't know, though I feel that it was judged well – but it really worked, and all my outfits up to now have been based on that bike. I didn't work from blueprints, it was all in my head, I just started with some steel tubing, and we got what turned out to be the best engine of that time in it, the 600cc Yamaha. By that time, having proved also that I could construct something that was safe, new parts started coming through from suppliers. That year, 1993, we cleaned up. The TT was ours for the taking. We were the quickest in practice and had the fastest lap in both races, lap records, race records, won the double, and it came easy. It all just fell together. It was an outstanding package that we put together that year, but I don't just mean the bike when I say that, I include Karl Ellison in there as well. He was probably the best available passenger at that time – he was possibly one of the best in the world back then, in fact – he was very good at it, and not only that, he's also a clever man, who's got a very good head on his shoulders; he was particularly good at analyzing things and talking things through after a race, which not every passenger is.

I only finished building the bike in the week running into the event. We did Jurby road circuit on the Saturday and won that, then we went out on Monday morning practice for the TT and were quickest instantly. It was all plain sailing with that bike. We literally strolled it. The first race we had a race record and a lap record. The second race again it was a stroll. It really was a very easy win. When I say it was easy, I mean that it didn't feel that fast after we had been riding Formula One machines a few years earlier. It's important to remember that those early Formula Two bikes were very slow compared to what we see now. They didn't accelerate like they do now, didn't corner like they do now, and they didn't have the top speed. But we were really delighted with that result, it was a major achievement; a double win for a start, but also I'd done it on my own bike, and from then on everybody wanted one. It was a turning point for me, as then I really got my teeth into building my own bikes and that's what got me race wins. I'm a good rider, but I'm not brilliant by any stretch of the imagination. However, I'm as good at building bikes as I am at riding, and together that's a successful combination.

It had taken us two years to get to grips with this new Formula Two class, but we did it. In 1991, the 600cc four-strokes had really started to come on. In 1991 Mick Boddice had won both races on a 600cc Honda; in 1992 Geoff Bell[11] did the same thing. In the solo classes the 600cc engine had really come on as well, so we knew which engine we wanted to use from then on. From the minute I rode on it, I knew we could win using it. The class had now developed to the point where we could see clearly which was the right engine to have, and this one engine dominated sidecars for the next five or six years, more so than any other engine. It was the basis of the modern Supersport 600cc engines, they were very fast and very powerful. Funnily enough, though, our main opposition back then came from Dave Saville, and he persevered with his old 350cc two-stroke. We put the lap record up from 102mph to 104mph that year and from memory he put his bike round at something like 102mph, so he was only a fraction behind us. But he'd got the absolute maximum out of that bike and it was obvious to everyone by then that the 350cc two-stroke was never going to compete at that level again, because the new generation of 600cc four-strokes which were coming along were far superior.

It was ironic in a way that the ACU had been leant on to get rid of the big bikes at the TT because they were too fast and too dangerous, which was true up to a point; it was an argument that you could legitimately make. So they changed it to Formula Two, and it reduced the speeds dramatically, by 7 or 8 miles an hour instantly, but then when they let the 600cc four-strokes in the speeds escalated so fast that by the time 1996 came, I'd broken the open class lap record by 2 or 3 miles an hour. Everybody thought Jock Taylor's lap record would stand for ever; well, in 1989 Mick Boddice just pipped it by a couple of seconds or so, at 108mph, then in 1996 I went round at 111mph, on a similar bike to the one we were running in 1993.

The 600cc Honda was a good engine, but it was a harder job to make it a fast engine than it was with the Yamaha equivalent. It was that bit more difficult, so for most people the Yamaha was the more favourable thing to use. You didn't really have to do a lot to it, it was fast straight away, whereas you had to do quite a bit of work to the Honda to make it a quick engine for a sidecar, and it was more expensive to do that as well. Boddice was a brilliant driver, and this combined with the fact that he had some very clever people working on his engines made him competitive. I remember having numerous dices with him throughout the 1993 season and into 1994, and he was a very hard man to beat on the track, but this competitive edge didn't last. The Yamahas came on a lot faster, along with the guys who were using them. There were soon more Yamahas on the grid than any other make. They were smaller engines as well, they were compact and they suited the chassis better, and also they were lower. From 1993 onwards, that Yamaha 600cc was *the* engine to use – certainly at the sharp end of the grid anyway. There were unexpected consequences of this – it got a lot more competitive in the paddock, for one thing. In the old days, anyone would have lent you a crank. From 1993 onwards you could still borrow bits from other competitors but it wasn't so easy – there was a lot more rivalry. Another unintended consequence was that although Formula Two rules had been introduced to try to lower the overall cost of the sport, and make it more cost-effective, it didn't work because it cost a lot more to make those modern four-stroke engines competitive. Those people with bigger budgets, or those who were willing to put their neck on the line with money, could make that road-bike engine into something pretty special. When you've got countries like the US running big race series using these engines, people will throw anything at it to make it faster and get more power out of it. If someone came to me and said, 'I've got five grand's worth of sponsorship, Dave,' I'd spend every last penny of that five grand, and more besides, to make my 600cc engine the best it could be.

Late on in 1993 Karl decided that he couldn't carry on passengering. He was in a career which was really taking off, and he had family commitments as well, so it was a shame. But I wanted to go racing off the Island more frequently, and he just couldn't carry on doing that with his other commitments. He's done really well for himself since, though. As luck would have it, I got Peter Hill on later that year. He had finished in second and third places behind us, riding with Eddie Wright, but they parted company around the same time that I lost Karl, so I wasn't treading on anyone's toes by teaming up with him. I rang Peter up and asked him if he wanted to come to the British Championship round at Brands Hatch with me at the end of the year, and he said yes right away. So we went off and didn't look back really; we gelled straight away. I was very lucky because I'd had Karl on for a few very good years, and he was second to none as a passenger. People like Peter Hill looked up to him, and I think it's fair to say that Peter probably learned a few things from Karl and took that with him, because it turned out that he was equally as good. He was an outstanding passenger, his ability to help steer the bike was just amazing. He always put himself in the right place at the right time. Peter is from Yorkshire, a very well-educated man, with a university degree, all the things you wouldn't really expect from a motorcycle racer, never mind a sidecar passenger!

In 1994 we went off to our first round of the British Championships, only a couple of weeks before the TT. We qualified in pole position, but we were lying second in the race when our engine blew up. It was a real setback. I felt that we should have won that round, but it was my own fault as I overcooked the engine and it did a crankshaft. Overall it was to be one of those years where nothing seemed to go right, especially after we'd had such a great year the previous year. The 1994 TT came around, and Rob Fisher[12] came with it! He was a great rider, in fact a bloody brilliant rider. We got stuck into that TT and we were damn quick, but Rob Fisher was quicker! He had done his homework and when he got to the TT he turned up the heat on us. He was quickest in practice, and I felt, 'Bloody hell, we've met our match here, definitely!' It was a bit of a shock as Rob was only a newcomer in 1993. We had thought that with our bike we were almost certainly staring a couple of wins in the face, but he put paid to that, and gave us a good kicking too! In more ways than one we had met our match, really, as he had a good bike, great engines and clever people around him. Rob was British Champion in Formula One, he'd done Grand Prix races, and he was a bloody talented rider. I think he may have started racing around the same time as me, in 1980 or 1981, we were similar ages, and I think he might even have raced at Flookburgh in the early days as well, so it was funny really how similar we were. In the 1994 TT I used the bike I had used the previous year, and that was probably my downfall, looking back on it. It genuinely was a case of resting on my laurels. I wasn't alone in thinking that the bike was not just good, but was *really* good. We were so far ahead of everyone else in 1993 that we felt we didn't need to improve it. But Rob came along and he won both races. The TT that year was a bit of a sad time. I was getting help in those days from the late Colin Aldridge, and Alan Smith who was one of his best pals, they were helping me out with my engines. Colin was a great sponsor of riders in the past. He sponsored Ray Swann, Kenny Irons and people like that, and this year he was sponsoring Mark Farmer. Colin was great, he used to call round to my garage all the time for a cuppa and a chat, we got on very well socially, and during practice week he brought Mark Farmer round to my garage to introduce him. We'd never met before but had a bit of a natter. He was a lovely lad, but he lost his life a couple of days later, and it affected Colin massively. He was very close to Mark.

The first sidecar race came along and Rob Fisher won it hands down. He used the same type of engine as me, so he was as least as good as me in terms of power. In the second race we went out and there was torrential rain for that event. We finished a good second again. We gave Rob a decent run for his money then, but we just couldn't match him. People have to understand that it's just not possible to put a wet-weather tyre on a sidecar and expect it to go to the end of a TT race, because it might be torrential rain like it was in that case for the first 7 miles, and then bone dry for the next 30 miles. That treaded tyre for the wet would be lucky to last just 7 wet miles, never mind complete three laps. So we had no choice but to put a hard slick on, something that we could go the full 113¾ miles on. We went off from the line at the start of that second race with slick tyres on, in wet conditions, and we charged off down Bray Hill; we'd no tyre warmers or anything like that, and the thing was aquaplaning down the entire length of Bray Hill. In that situation as a driver you're actually just a passenger yourself; you're on a sledge and you're not in control!

That second race I rode my heart out, I absolutely did, and at the time I felt I went a bit near the edge. The speeds don't reflect that when you're talking in today's terms because of the high speeds we're doing today. But I was riding that bike as hard as I do today; in fact harder than I do today. You still go around corners at the same speed, and when I feel like I've gone that bit too far, I do question myself afterwards; I sometimes get a bit upset with myself and it was true in that case. I felt I'd ridden hard, maybe too hard, to try and win this race, but it didn't work. I did get upset and I remember someone, I think maybe it was Mick Boddice who finished third, leaning over to me and saying, 'Christ, Dave, it's nothing to get upset about!' He thought I was upset about finishing second, but it wasn't that at all. It had all just got me thinking about being introduced to Mark Farmer and how his death had affected Colin. Sometimes that gets you thinking about all the other people you knew who've died racing, and I just questioned myself for a split second. I thought, 'Fuck me, I took that too far.' I still would have finished second, even if I hadn't tried so hard, but I tried that bit too much. I remember I was openly upset, and it was noted, and some people might have read it like I was a bad loser, or that I was pissed off that I'd finished second. Well, it wasn't that at all. I wasn't in the slightest bit pissed off because I'd finished second. I was, however, pissed off with myself, that I'd put my and my passenger's necks on the chopping block just to get that second place.

The fact that I rode so hard, combined with the emotions of the week, made it a delicate sort of time really. I was proud of the results that I gained, as I always am. I don't particularly care where I finish so long as I know I've tried my bloody hardest. I did that, and I lost to a better man that day. That was it. The fact was, it was slightly misinterpreted at the time but, again, that's as much my fault as anyone else's. So often in these cases I'm guilty of not expressing what I'm thinking or feeling in the way that I really want to. It's either because the timing isn't right because I'm about to start a bloody race in one minute's time, or the opportunity isn't there because a commentator wants a ten-second sound bite, and so these myths and misapprehensions grow up around me. It's partly through incidents like that, that this whole 'Moody Moly' thing grew up, and maybe this book is my opportunity to put the record straight in a lot of areas where I haven't got across what I really meant in the past.

The following week we went off to Donington Park in Leicestershire, to the British Championship round, and we qualified in pole again. I got a dreadful start in the race itself, I was last away because they were push starts in those days. Gary Smith went on to win the race, I was second, and Rob Fisher was third. Rob and I had had a good dice through that event, I'd caught him up and passed him, and so I felt good about that! Things went well for a few meetings after that. We won at Oulton Park, the British Championship round, but the round after that I didn't finish the race because I broke down. The last round of the British Championship that year was at Brands Hatch and I bumped into Steve Hislop[13] there. I knew Steve of old, I'd known him since 1989 and my first TT win, and he was a really nice bloke, a spade's-a-spade kind of fellow. It was the Thursday night and I was due to go out on the Friday for the practice session, but my passenger wasn't able to make it because he had to work that day. So I was down at the bar getting something to eat when I met Steve. He was riding for the Castrol Honda team at the time. Things hadn't gone well for Hislop that year. He was on the RC45 and he had struggled with it all that season. He was due to practise the following day as well, but I told him that I couldn't go out without a passenger. My regular guy, Peter Hill, couldn't make it and I couldn't just get someone on the sidecar with me without a licence. Hislop said, 'Ah stuff it, I'll get on with you, I've always wanted to have a go.' Well, it was true, he did have a competition licence, but I was more worried about what Honda would think of it! Shaking my head, I said, 'You can't get on that sidecar with me, what if you fall off the back of it, you'll be hung, drawn and quartered by your team!' Steve said, 'D'you know what, I don't give a shit, because I'll be sacked after this meeting anyway!' I told him that in that case we were first out the next morning, at half past nine. He said, 'I'll be there.'

So the next morning he came walking down the paddock, still wearing his knee sliders and all the kit you wear on a solo. I said, 'Bloody hell, you'll have to rip those knee pads off or you'll be skating all over the sidecar platform.' 'While we're at it,' I told him, 'I don't think you *should* move, really. If you just kneel in the middle of the bike while I just go round in circles and get this engine run in, that'll do me.' 'Aye, no problem Dave.' So I think I did something like twenty laps in total, and about ten laps in I thought I would pick the pace up a bit, but first I looked over my left shoulder to see if Steve was comfortable. I looked round and he wasn't bloody there! I panicked and thought, 'Oh for fuck's sake, he's fallen off the back of it!' That was a split-second reaction, and then I looked over my right shoulder and there he was, hanging over the back wheel of the bike like a full professional passenger, giving me the thumbs up and obviously loving it! So I gave it a bit more gas and actually the time we went round in would have qualified us halfway up the grid. Considering he'd never done it in his life before, that was very good. But after twenty laps he gave me a tap on the back and we pulled into the pit lane. He was puffing and panting, and he was well exhausted, but he was getting into all sorts of odd shapes that you wouldn't normally get into as a passenger; he didn't quite know how to do it. In fact, when he was hanging out for a left-hand corner, he actually had his knee out of the bike. I don't know how he managed it, and I remember that at the time I thought, 'Fucking hell, that must be uncomfortable!' But he told me afterwards, 'I would do that again any day, Dave, you've got to give me another go!' Hislop was a great bloke, a really nice guy, and he did go on and win his round of the British Championships that weekend! I wish I'd got him out on a sidecar again but the opportunity just never came around, it never happened that we were in the right place at the right time.

That weekend was going to decide the British Sidecar Championship for 1994. I had to win to stand a chance of taking it. Mick
Boddice and Geoff Bell were tied on points ahead of me, but there
were only a few points in it. I had to win, but also Boddice and Bell
had to finish a lot further down the order for me to clinch it. I went
on and won the race; it was a fantastic ride, I got a great start which
was unusual for me, and we were first into Paddock Hill bend. It was
damp that day but we just followed a dry line which had been laid
down by the previous solo race earlier in the day. So I followed this
and I ended the first lap out five seconds in the lead while all the rest
were bumping and barging on a damp track somewhere behind me,
and I won it by something ridiculous like ten seconds. I lost the
British Championship, though, by one point, and that was the nearest
I got to winning that title. Some of it was my own fault, with things
like engine blow-ups, but in other things we were just unlucky. We did
try, though, and it was a damn good end to a hard season.

Back home, in the week running up to Christmas 1994, I got a phone
call from a guy with an American accent, who told me that he was a
video art film-maker, and he wanted to include me in a film that he
was planning to make. I thought it was someone taking the piss, one
of my mates perhaps, and I told him that I thought he was winding
me up. I was about to put the phone down on him, but he assured me
that he wasn't, and he asked for my address so he could send me some
information. A couple of days later this FedEx parcel turned up with
all this literature and bits and bobs in it, telling me who he was and
what he did, and telling me about the ideas he had for this forty-five-
minute film that he wanted to make. It turned out he was a guy called
Matthew Barney, who had been in London the previous year seeking
funding for his art movies. He was going to go to Southern Ireland
looking for filming locations, because he was interested in scenery
with yellow gorse in it and so on, when someone suggested that he go
to the Isle of Man as well. So he had jumped on a plane and came over

during the 1993 TT, and saw Karl Ellison and myself win the sidecar double. He was very taken with sidecars, he'd never seen anything like this before, and he decided that he wanted to include them in his film. He called them 'Hacks'!

He chose to make his film here, and he got permission from the Isle of Man Government to close roads and so on, so that he could shoot this thing properly, and he wanted me to help him. I thought, 'Well, it beats spraying cars for a fortnight', and I also had an idea that it might be a bit of a laugh. I'd been asked to organize getting another sidecar in, and I knew that a lad who was working for me at the time on motorcycle bodywork, Karl Sinnott, had a dad who raced sidecars at the TT, Steve Sinnott. They were good friends of mine, the pair of them, so I thought I'll get them to ride one sidecar, and me and my brother Graham will ride the other. There was some sort of colour theme going on in this movie, so Karl and Steve rode the blue bike, and we rode the yellow bike. I got a lot of work out of this: I had to produce new bodywork for the two bikes, and spray them in these colours, and I even got Manx Leathers the work of making the race suits we wore, and some of the other garments people in the movie wore. I also made props and other bits and pieces for use in the film.

We had two weeks of real good fun – it was another world. These people who come from a movie background are quite outrageous! I knew this guy Matthew Barney was on the edge; a wild-looking character, but a lovely bloke, in fact all the people involved with that film were lovely people, and a pleasure to work with. But I remember one night we were all having a few drinks and a bit of a laugh and someone was comparing tattoos, then someone else had a piercing that they were showing off. Then Matthew said, 'Well, look at this,' and he dropped his trousers, and his bollocks were pierced about half a dozen times! I said, 'For fuck's sake, what's that all about!!' He went, 'You'll see later as the movie develops!' Sure enough, on the very last day of filming we were on the Queen's Pier in Ramsey, which they had spent thousands of pounds decorating. They had decked out the old pavilion on the end really nicely (in fact they should have left it like that!). There was a stage there, shaped like a pair of bollocks. A set of strings were laid out from the two sidecars for about 30 feet towards this stage. All of a sudden, up jumps Matthew Barney on there, drops his trousers and connects these bloody strings to his bollocks! Well, I was wetting myself laughing at this point because Karl and Steve were up in arms. They said, 'You never told us he was some kind of fucking pervert!!' Matthew said, 'Come on lads, this is serious, you've got to slowly draw the strings in until they become taut!' 'Fuck off, you dirty bastard!' they were shouting at him! Well, it was March, it was freezing cold, and there was Matthew standing there with his tackle out – well, it wasn't all out, because it was half covered in latex, so you couldn't see everything – but you could certainly get the gist of it! Eventually I managed to get the guys calmed down. I said, 'Come on, you aren't going to be looked at any worse for doing this, think of all the other weird shots we've done this week!' Christ, it was just hilarious at the time.

A couple of days after the filming finished, Matthew had a few things still to tie up and he phoned me at the garage. He asked if Steve was still on the Island, because he knew he lived in Peterborough. I told him that he was staying on for another week. He then asked if all four of us could get down to the Queen's Pier later that day. We were really busy so I was reluctant to go, but he told us, 'I'll make it worth your while, I'll give you £200 each for literally five minutes' work.' Quick as a flash I said, 'We'll be there!' So we had to put our leathers and the other kit on when we got down to the pier. It turned out that a photographer, a lady called Annie Leibovitz, who was at the time one of the most famous photographers connected to the movie world, was in London that week. I think she was covering some Planet Hollywood opening or something. Someone told her that Matthew Barney was making this film on the Isle of Man, and suggested that she go over to see what he was doing. Her people must have phoned him to arrange this, and she flew over, got a taxi straight up to Ramsey along with all her kit and about half a dozen hangers-on, took pictures of us, and then went off straight away! It was all over and done in minutes, but these pictures appeared in *Vogue* magazine the following month; pictures of us guys stood on the Queen's Pier with our leathers on, male modelling! I got loads of other work off Matthew. Six months later I made him some replicas of the bikes we had used – just full-sized mock-ups with the bodywork on – and I crated them up and then they were air-freighted out to America where he has a gallery and a permanent show on. It was one of life's experiences that was just brilliant, and he did pay us really well. It was a good thing to be involved in. He also sponsored us a little, he paid for our race fuel for that year's TT, for Steve Sinnott and myself. He was a real nice guy, and I'd like to meet him again at some point. He went on to marry Bjork, the pop singer, and I think he lives in New York now. That film he made became a sort of cult thing, it's called *Cremaster 4*; you can find it if you look it up on the internet, and I'm there on the cast list!

In 1995 I really got into racing on the European scene. That year I was doing the European Championships with a bike that was put together on the smallest of budgets. I hired the engine from Dennis Trollope, who supplied racing spares. It was a Krauser engine, a 500cc two-stroke, four-cylinder model. It was a little bit dated, it was probably five years out of date in fact, but it was still competitive enough for the European Championships. I also built a chassis, using a short-wheelbase layout. That was a type that no one else was really using any more, and it did raise some eyebrows! We went to Assen for the Dutch round of the European Championships, which was the first one, in March 1995, and we qualified in pole position. It was quite funny really, as the scrutineers were actually laughing at this bike I had built. They thought it was a classic bike, because it was basically the same as a Formula Two bike is today, which in turn is based on a design from thirty years ago, but it had a modern engine in it. People back then underestimated the handling capabilities of a Formula Two bike that was put together right. Even though we couldn't really afford to keep good tyres on it, and it wasn't aerodynamically that great, it was *really* fast. You could get that thing round corners outrageously fast. We really pissed on their parade! We went out and qualified in pole, and they *hated* it, they really hated the fact that we had put this thing on pole position! We went out in the race itself, and we led that for a time, but we developed a misfire and after a while we were running on just two cylinders. We dropped back and eventually finished in sixth place. Afterwards this Scottish guy called Mike Clark came running up to us in the paddock, full of excitement, saying, 'I watched you on that thing, it was like a cart going round corners compared to those big bikes, what went wrong with it?' I said, 'Oh, the ignition broke.' 'How much is an ignition?' 'About seven hundred quid,' and he wrote me a cheque for £700 there and then. I'd never met this guy from Adam, and there he was giving us a cheque for that amount of money! He was in such a hurry that day that I never even got his phone number to start with!

The next event that year was the Isle of Man TT. I was still planning to use my bike, the one I had won the double there on in 1993. I had updated it slightly, I'd put a new engine in it, but the truth is that in 1995 I was so hell-bent on trying to break into European and World Championship racing that it really did cost us dearly at the TT. I think that year I had really spread myself very thinly. I still felt that the 1993 bike was capable of winning, the engines we had were capable and we were definitely capable of it, but my efforts had been sorely stretched by chasing this European dream. I had been so desperate to get in there and prove myself, for a number of years by that point, that to some extent I thought, 'This time the TT will just have to look after itself.' All of my available finances had been channelled into that European bid. I suppose I was guilty once again of resting on my laurels a bit where the TT was concerned, but in reality I had few other options open to me. I had other things going on as well that year. I had built Rob Fisher a new bike in the winter of 1994/95, and he crashed it in the Thursday afternoon practice of that 1995 TT. He came to me on the Friday with a bike that was nearly bent in half, and said to me, 'Dave, can you fix it for me?' It was a real dilemma for me: I'd built the bike for him, and so I was kind of obliged to fix it. But at the same time he was my nearest rival. We were both fiercely competitive. We were friends, don't get me wrong about that, but that all definitely stopped once the TT started each year! In spite of that (or perhaps because of that) if I had said 'No' to him, then I'd have been the biggest twat in the world. But the real problem was I honestly didn't have the *time* to fix it. I had my own issues with my own bike to sort out, because it had developed an electrical fault and we just couldn't trace it. But my back was up against the wall; I had to do this for Rob, mainly because I felt that if I didn't fix it for him, and if I then went out and won, it would not have been a genuine victory in a way. So I fixed his bike, but I fell so far behind with my own machine that I never even started the first race. My bike was still in bits, and I didn't even make the grid.

We were ready and we went out for the second race, and that was a saga all in itself. We were in the warming-up area, all full of confidence and fired up to hell. We were going to get one back on Rob, or so we thought. We started the bike, and it only ran on three cylinders. I thought, 'Christ, what's going on here?', so in a panic, because there were only five minutes to go to the start of the race, we took the seat off, replaced all the spark plugs and it ran on all four cylinders again. We thought, 'Great!' We put the seat back on, and pushed the machine up to the start line. The 3-minute board came up, and I sat on the bike. As I did so, the kneeling tray on the right-hand side of the seat sank down. I looked under it, and saw that it hadn't gone back into its locating peg when we had put the seat back. My brother by this time had gone off to the pit area, and I didn't have a screwdriver to get the seat off. So I lay under the bike, and I had to use both my thumbs to lever the carbon-kevlar bodywork over the peg. As I did so, I dislocated my left thumb. It was literally bent back touching my wrist. I yelled out, 'Aaagh!!! Fucking hell!' We were there on the start line, about to race, and the 2-minute board now came up. Peter Hill pulled my glove off, and there was a blue crease around the base of my thumb where it was dislocated. He said to me, 'Dave, you can't ride like that!' I yelled back, 'I can!' I put my hands between my legs, yanked my thumb and felt it go back into its socket, put my glove straight back on and off I went for the start of the race! It happened literally that fast! I thought to myself, 'This is just a fucking *disaster*! Everything is against us this year. This is just not meant to be!' So I had all these stupid thoughts in my head, wondering if I should carry on, and worrying for most of the first lap that if the handlebars got into a wobble it would push my thumb back out of its socket. We carried on, but the front brake master cylinder failed, which supplied the front discs, so we then only had a back brake and sidecar wheel brake. That was halfway round and we nearly went straight on at Ramsey Hairpin as a result, but still we finished second. It was a good second, a strong second, but I thought, 'Thank Christ that's all over.' We had had a heavy week, a hell of a week in fact, but after it was all over Rob thanked me for fixing his bike! I was glad that he won, though, because I'd built a bike for someone who had gone on to win the TT with it – twice.

Following the TT, our next racing event in 1995 turned out to be a rather unexpected one. After the Assen European Championship round everyone was talking about the bike we had used, because it was quite exciting to see a conventional short-wheelbase bike competing against the long-wheelbase machines. Everybody had written off the short-wheelbase bike as an uncompetitive package years ago, but now we had turned all that thinking around at that level. So it was because of all this interest that Billy Nutt, who was promoting the Ulster Grand Prix at that time, rang me up. He said, 'Dave, we'd like to see you at the Ulster Grand Prix.' He knew I wasn't keen on the idea, but he carried on all the same, 'I know all about the past, but just come over and have a look. I'll give you a bit of start money, that will cover your boat fares, and really you should win it as that's a great little bike you've got. You could go away with a nice little pay packet on your hip.' He was quite persuasive, so in the end I thought, 'What the hell, I'll go and do it.'

My objections to racing at Dundrod were not based solely on the fact that my father was killed there. It was a long circuit – from memory it's about 7 miles long, and that's a hard circuit to learn. I wasn't really accustomed to going to a long circuit and being a newcomer. But the bottom line was that it felt strange going there, after what I associated with the Ulster Grand Prix, and it turned out to be the only time that I ever went to that event. We had a great team then, there was Norman Burgess, who comes from a racing background going back to the year dot. He's from Clitheroe and his father, brothers and he all raced with some considerable success. Norman had an accident and sustained serious injuries in the 1989 Sidecar TT second leg, enough to put him out of racing for good, but he still has a great passion for the sport. He's one of those great characters that you meet in life that are just amazing. Through 1995 and 1996 he was involved with me, he got us some sponsorship and came to all of the race meetings with us. He was a great guy to have around. When spirits were down, he got them up again, he was the joker of the pack. We also had Mike Clark, who had just started sponsoring us, and my brother Graham. So off we all went to Northern Ireland, where an ex-policeman named Lewis had offered us accommodation. We stayed at his house and he gave us an old Morris Minor with flick-out indicators to get around in. We turned up at the event, and we were the last team to arrive, just the night before. On the morning of the practice sessions, just before the roads closed at lunchtime, we took out this Morris Minor, with Peter Hill in the passenger seat, and my brother Graham and Mike Clark in the back. Off we went round the Ulster Grand Prix circuit, the first time

I'd ever been around the course! On the fourth lap round, the car threw a big end. It was clanking like an old tin can. We were doing 80 miles an hour down the Flying Kilo and 'bang!' it went. I thought, 'Fuck, I've wrecked Lewis's car!' So we limped back to the paddock, had a good laugh about that, and then went out to practice that afternoon. We qualified for pole position instantly. It was exciting; I just seemed to slot into it straight away. It was our third lap of practice when we set our pole time. In the second practice session we went out and on the first lap another big end went, this time it was on my race bike, so we sat out the rest of that practice session. We got back to the paddock, fitted a new crankshaft and put a new cylinder in it, and went out for the race the next day.

It was all good fun, up to that point; the weather was great, everything seemed to be going well, but it turned out to be a sad do. An old friend of ours, Marty Murphy, was in the same race as us, dicing for third position when he crashed and lost his life. Close to the end of the race we got a red flag and came in, but nobody knew why. On the same lap there was another crash, but we knew those people were OK, so nobody knew at first why the race had been stopped. We finished in first place, and unfortunately the garlanding ceremony went ahead. We went up on the rostrum, everyone was having a laugh with champagne and garlands, all that crap, and we had just come back down to the paddock that the news came through that Marty had lost his life. So that was a shitty thing, to say the least. There didn't seem to be anything else to do, so we thought, let's go and get a pint. By the time we got down to the beer tent that was shut, so things were just getting better and better.

On our way back from the beer tent, one of the weirdest things ever happened to me. As we were on our way back to the paddock, some guy stopped me and said, 'Are you Dave Molyneux?' I answered, 'Yeah, why?' He said, 'Christ, I've been waiting to see you for a long time. I've got something for you.' And he reached inside his coat and pulled out a piece of bodywork with the Three Legs of Man painted on it. It turned out that this had been painted by my dad, on the side of his fairing, before the crash. When this fellow had bought his house, it had been nailed up on one of the roof joists in his garage. He asked what it was all about and was told that in 1977 two Manx lads had been in an accident and had been killed nearby. It turned out that when my dad had crashed at Tournagrough, this piece of bodywork had been thrown into the field behind the house. The previous owner of the place had picked it up and put it in the garage with a nail through the centre of the Three Legs. The guy who gave the piece to me had started following the bikes as a result of this, and he began asking questions – 'Doesn't Dave Molyneux ever race here?' – because he'd heard of me, he knew who I was, and got told, 'No.' Then when he'd heard that I was finally coming to the event that year, he pulled it off the beam and gave it to me. I've still got it, it's one of the most emotive things I'll ever own.

I couldn't afford to do every round of the European Championships that year. I think the next round would have been at Schleiz in Germany, and we didn't do that one, which was a shame as it was a road circuit, and that chassis would have been awesome around there. The next round we did do was at Most in the Czech Republic, but the heat there was horrendous. It must have been 90 degrees. The track temperature there was as if it was on fire. We just couldn't keep a front tyre in the bike because after three laps it was just shredded, it was overheated to hell. The tyre supplier at Most didn't have a hard enough rubber compound to cope with the heat, of a type that fitted our bike. He was catering for the bigger Formula One bikes and their tyres just didn't fit ours. It was something else that we learned on the way. In practice we qualified in pole position once again; it was absolutely on fire, was that bike. It was fantastically fast. During that session we tailed the guy who eventually went on to win the race down the start–finish straight, which goes into a right-hand kink and then a big fast fifth-gear left-hander, and I just rode right round the outside of him like he was in another gear. His bike was on another plane and my passenger, Peter Hill, was looking behind him, giving this guy the thumbs up as we went by! It was bloody brilliant! In the race itself, though, we had to pull out before the end. The front tyre overheated so badly that it was like it had marbles underneath it, and we had no choice but to retire.

The next European Championship event that season was at Donington Park. I think we qualified in pole position there as well, if not then it was second. We did the distance this time: we finished third in that race, which was a great result for us. We'd discovered that the bike needed lots of work doing to it to be competitive in that class, really, but it was all work that was definitely achievable. If I'd had the technology that I've got today in that bike, it would probably have won the World Championship, easily! It had the makings of a really good bike. I think we then went on to the Jock Taylor Memorial meeting at Knockhill, and we had a second and a first there, but that was it for us for that season. We'd spent up – we'd had a great run of European meetings, and we'd fitted the Ulster Grand Prix in as well that year – so all in all it had been a pretty hectic season.

Chapter 3

Leader of the Pack

About a month after the end of the 1995 racing season, I think it was in November of 1995, the organizer of the European Championships rang me up to ask if I was intending to enter again the following year. I said yes I was, and he told me in that case I needed to get a more up-to-date bike. I told him that I was updating the bike I had, and that I knew what I had to do to it to make it a winner. He responded, 'No, we won't accept that bike in the class next year.' I was puzzled by this and I asked him why, what was against it? It was a sidecar, for God's sake, and it had a 500cc two-stroke engine just like you could use in any other World Championship event. He replied that the organizers didn't want the little bike, with the short wheelbase, back at the series. I still didn't clock on, and asked again what was against it. His answer really stunned me, he said, 'The other competitors are against it ...' I thought, 'Right ... OK ...' And that was that. As far as I was concerned, I was walking away from the European Championships. For the first time in a long while I got my head down between November and about February and worked like buggery. As a result, I had a decent bank balance for the first time in ages. I thought, 'Bloody hell, this is good, I might just do the TT this coming year and leave it at that.' Work was good, business was booming, plenty of car jobs were coming in for spraying, and then out of the blue Mike Clark, who had bought us the ignition the previous year, rang me up. He asked what I was doing racing-wise for the coming season. I said, 'I'm doing nothing, Mike. I might just do the TT. I've got a bike half-put-together here. I've got a good engine in my workshop which I've managed to obtain. Failing that, I'm doing nothing.' He was slightly surprised by this answer, and he asked why. So I told him what had happened: 'They've banned the bike, so I've cut the front off it and turned it into a 600cc bike for the TT. It's halfway between a European Championship bike and a TT bike at the moment!' Without a pause Mike said, 'Well, I've got ten grand here burning a hole in my pocket, would that be enough to buy a chassis, if Dennis Trollope will hire us an engine again like last year?' I couldn't say yes fast enough! I was straight on the phone to Terry Windle,[14] who was building great chassis at the time; he had Darren Dixon[15] and Steve Abbott on his chassis. Darren had just won a World Championship on one of his machines, so I thought, 'We'll have one of them!' I rang Terry up and it just so happened he had a second-hand chassis in for some repairs, and it was … £10,000! So that put paid to the ten grand. Then I blew most of the money I had earned over the winter on it as well. I put new bodywork on the thing, hired the engine from Dennis Trollope, and that was us into the 1996 European Championship season.

The first round was at Assen in Holland like the previous year. This now called for a completely different style of riding to the one I had really come to call my own. In fact, it was shockingly different to what I was used to. It was a completely different bike, because it had a 500cc two-stroke engine in a long-wheelbase monocoque-built Formula One chassis. So it was a whole new ball-game; the only resemblance to a TT bike was that it had three wheels! It took quite a bit of adapting to, as you can imagine! But we qualified in pole position again, instantly, and I thought, 'Yep, pissed on your parade again!' The doubters had all thought we wouldn't be able to adapt our style to ride one of these big Formula One bikes, but we did, and not only that, we qualified in pole position. Incidentally, we only went at about the same speed as we had done the previous year on my own chassis, so that was satisfying. It showed the potential that bike might have had. Unfortunately, on the next-to-last lap of the race at Assen, the eighteenth lap, the engine blew up. So not only did we fail to finish, we were also faced with a big bill to repair it. Luckily Norman Burgess, Mike Clark and a few other lads chipped in and we got enough money together to fix the engine. We went on to Donington, to the British Championship race, in which I think we finished in sixth place.

Then the 1996 Isle of Man TT came around, and we cleaned up. We absolutely bloody buried it. We knocked the record book for six. We had Slick Bass helping us that year. Slick was Carl Fogarty's crew chief in the four World Championships that he won, but he had just lost his job with Honda that year and was now back home in Ramsey. I asked him if he would tune our engine for the TT. He came down and helped us out, and did a great job. The existing lap record for Formula Two machines at the TT was 107 miles an hour in Rob Fisher's name, and the Formula One lap record was 108 miles an hour in Mick Boddice's name, and we lapped at 110 miles an hour on the first night of practice! The thing was, we hadn't even ridden that bike on a circuit before. Before the TT we took it up the Jurby airfield straight, and I think it was on the third run up and down the straight that I decided the bike was probably as good as it was ever going to be. I came back in after that run and told my brother, 'I think we can go one tooth bigger on the gearing at the back, and that will do it. Other than that, the bike feels pretty good.' Peter Hill agreed, and that was really all the preparation work we did on that bike. On the first night of TT practice, the Monday night, we did a 107 mile an hour lap from a standing start and 110 miles an hour on the second lap. We just blew the paddock apart. They couldn't believe it. Talk about moving the goalposts, that sent them into another age. I came in, and I knew it was good but I didn't know just how good. Actually, it was quite hard for me to judge. I hadn't ridden a short-wheelbase bike for some time, and I was more used to the speeds on European Championship bikes.

The machine I was using was a lot better than any I had ridden before at the TT, by a long chalk. It was the bike that I'd had the Krauser engine in, when I'd done the European circuits the previous year; I'd cut the thing in half, and put a whole new front on it to accommodate a 600cc Yamaha engine. It was better than anything else partly due to the fact that we ran wider wheels in the European Championship races, and I left those on it for the TT. The accepted thinking in those days was that narrower wheels were better for the TT. As usual, money played a big part in the decision-making process. I didn't have the funds to change the wheels, so in the end I thought, 'Sod it, I'll just have to get bigger tyres.' So we went up from an 8-inch to 10-inch-wide back wheel and it really improved the steering. Kind of by accident I found a good formula between that and my chassis. Also the updated FZR600 engine, which was a newer generation engine, was a lot better than what we had used before. We had nothing trick on it. It was a standard CDI ignition pack, which only revved to 12,000rpm, as opposed to today's 17,000rpm unit. It was carburettored, it didn't have an air box on it. It was so basic it was quite untrue, but Slick did a fantastic job on the engine, and the combination of that and the chassis we had put together just sent it into another world.

We came in after that first practice, and Peter had had a rough ride. He said to me, 'Jesus, Dave, that was the worst ride I've ever had round here. I don't know what speed we did but it nearly shook me to bits.' The back suspension was a bit alien to us – we'd had no run-up to the event, no time to test it – so it was a bit too solid, too stiff on the back. Poor old Peter had got a right old shaking. His gums were bleeding; his chin was cut where he had caught it on the passenger handles, keeping his head down out of the wind. It had also taken all the skin off his shins. But he was a hard man was Peter, he was probably one of the best in the business. He was a 'not-give-in' kind of guy. He would never hit me on the back and stop me, not for anything. When we did stop that night he was quite angry really, but then at that point my brother came running over to us with a stopwatch, shouting, 'You're not going to believe this, but you've just done over 110 miles an hour!' I said, 'No, you've got it wrong!' Well, my brother never gets it wrong. He's as good a timekeeper as any in the country, in the world probably. He said, 'No, I'm telling you, you've just lapped at over 110 miles an hour!' and I still laugh now when I think about Peter's reaction to that. He turned round to us without blinking and said, 'Well, no fucking wonder my shins are bleeding!!'

It was a different story when we pushed the bike back down to the paddock, it was like someone had died. It was very sombre. The rest of the paddock had faces like slapped arses, which was a bit of a shock, really. Maybe it shouldn't have been, but it was. Nobody patted us on the back, nobody said 'Well done, Dave' or 'Well done, Peter, you've just made history', nothing like that at all. So we put the bike in the van and we went home. We only had one good engine, so we only did four laps of practice that week. But we came up to the Grandstand for the next practice session, and in scrutineering we were asked for a fuel sample. I said to the scrutineers, 'Why do you want a fuel sample in the *second* practice session?' Then the penny dropped, how stupid could I be. They thought we were cheating. I'd heard the whispers going around, that we had a big bore engine in, that it was impossible for a Formula Two bike to go that fast, and that we had to be cheating. Anyone who knows me knows that if I'm accused of cheating it's like a red rag to a bull, big time. But these slurs were coming from people I really admired, and people who I had grown up admiring. I just thought, how pathetic and small-minded. They know I'm a decent rider. They know I can build a decent machine. What makes them think this achievement can't be genuine? Even if I *had* been cheating and had a big bore engine in, then I had *still* broken the record for that engine by over 2 miles an hour, so that was an achievement in itself! I was gutted, I really was. I was so angry I could have packed the whole thing in and gone home there and then. I felt that bad that they thought I would do something like that on my home soil. If I had been cheating, I would have been caught out almost straight away anyway, and then I wouldn't have been able to walk into the local shop to buy a Mars bar without being ashamed of myself. It was pure envy, pure green-eyed jealousy, that created that situation. I had never been accused of cheating before. I'd won lots of races previously. They knew my ability as a driver. They knew Peter's ability as a passenger, and they knew I had a damn good bike under me, so I was bloody pissed off, to put it mildly. Not one of my fellow competitors said, 'Well done Dave', and I found that pretty hurtful. That's the truth.

In those days, in scrutineering, the top of your engine had to come off. They would measure the cylinder bore and stroke, measure the size of the carburettor, and they would test your fuel. When I got asked for that fuel on the Tuesday night, I said, 'I'll save you some hassle. That's Premium Unleaded and it came from Kirk Michael filling station.' It's important to remember that just prior to that, the ACU had banned leaded race fuel in some vain attempt at being green and friendly to the atmosphere, or some such shit. In the years previous to that, in 1993 and 1994, we had been using full-on, leaded, 118-octane high-performance race fuel. It was damned dangerous if it wasn't handled carefully, and expensive as well. But they banned this stuff, and it took a few years before high-octane unleaded race fuel became available, so basically for the time being we had to use fuel from a roadside pump. To cap it all, they didn't actually have Super Unleaded in garages on the Isle of Man at that point! So what we were using was the cheapest shit that you would have put in your old Vauxhall Viva! That was what was in that tank. And the following night when I went up to practice the scrutineers looked a bit sheepish and said to me, 'Yeah, Dave, that fuel was what you said it was.' I just shook my head, and laughed.

We won the first race, and set the first ever 110 mile an hour lap officially then. That's always pissed me off as well, the way they say that. Why is it not official on a practice? It's the same timekeepers using the same stopwatches! Today it's done with transponders so you can't get it wrong! That's always ground me out has that, that you can set a lap record in practice but it's not recognized as such. But that's beside the point. We won the race, and one of the scrutineers came over and said, 'Do you want me to tag your engine, Dave?' That means they drill the cylinder head bolts, and they put a lockwire through it and a lead seal. They then let you race in the second race if that seal is intact, but if the seal is broken you would be excluded. I said, 'No, I don't want it tagged. Get that thing in the scrutineering bay and let's have the cylinder head off as quickly as we can.' So off to the scrutineering bay we went, and there must have been thirty vultures hovering who just couldn't wait to see it fail. They must have been absolutely *gagging* to see that thing declared illegal in some way or form. Well, we pissed on their parade as well! If the truth be known, and Slick would testify to this, that engine was actually quite a pile of shit. He made it a good engine, but only through his ability as an engine tuner. It was not a good engine in itself, and he didn't think it would last, that's how poor it was. It was down to me that it was rubbish, I didn't have the money to put the bits in it, but he put some TLC into it and that got it home.

Anyway, that shut up all the backstabbers. It was legal and that was that. We went out for the second race and I was determined we were going to average over 110 miles an hour for the three laps on this one, never mind lap at it. And we did, we averaged over 110 miles an hour. We put the lap record up to over 111 miles an hour, and that was back in 1996. There are people today who struggle to do that speed, and I would say the track is 3 miles an hour faster today, easily. I sold the bike immediately. In fact a guy came to me wanting to buy that bike before the second race – after it had been declared all above board obviously! – but we agreed a price, he gave me a cheque, and I remember coming down towards the Creg on the last lap of the second race thinking, 'Keep going you bastard thing!!' It sounded like a bag of nuts and bolts! He bought that thing as seen, with no spares or anything, but I told him in no uncertain terms, 'You definitely need to get that engine rebuilt before you run it!' Well, he couldn't resist it – he went out to Oulton Park the following week, for a short circuit meeting and on his sixth lap the bloody con rod snapped and went out the front of the engine. A history-making engine destroyed, all because he couldn't be patient! Funnily enough, though, that bike is now out in New Zealand, a guy is running it out there, and it's still winning races after all these years.

But we picked up a good pay-packet at that TT. I sold my bike for what was probably a record amount. I just named my price, and the guy said, 'I'm having it and that's all there is to it.' He had plenty of money by the sound of it, and he bought the bike. Combined with my prize money, that meant I was sitting on about twenty grand altogether. I was at another crossroads in my life. I thought, 'Well, I've got two choices here. I could buy a spray booth for my business, and that could send me into the future with a good income by upping my game in my work, or I could head off to Europe to go racing instead.' I was still pissed off, though, about what had happened at the TT that year. I'm a bit of a prick when it comes to being affected by what other people say, think or do, and with all that shit that had been slung at me, I thought, 'Well, we took that TT to a different level, broke all the records, and if someone else wants to have all that now they're welcome to it.' I wanted to go somewhere else. So I decided that the twenty grand or more that we'd won was going to go on racing elsewhere. The second race at the 1996 TT was delayed due to rain, so to get off the Isle of Man quickly we chartered a small plane, an air taxi, and flew to Blackpool, where my friend Norman Burgess met us with our race truck and our Formula One bike. We then drove for two days, non-stop almost, down to Rome, to Vallelunga in Italy. It was the Italian round of the European Championships and we had a great race there. We qualified in pole position again, and we finished second to a local guy called Galbiati. It was a great week, probably one of the best weeks of my life in racing terms. We'd just had this outstanding performance at the TT, then a great result in this European Championship round. Into the bargain, while we were there, we managed to source a Honda ADM engine, which was *the* engine to have at the time; Darren Dixon had just won the World Championship on one. The following week we got in a car and drove all the way down to Switzerland, Norman Burgess, myself, Mike Clark the sponsor and Mark Barker, who was helping out with the engine by doing a bit of spannering. We paid £14,000 for this second-hand engine. I thought it was bloody fantastic. We had a wild night out, a proper lads' night out in Basel, celebrating the fact that we'd got this engine, and thinking, 'Right, now we're on our way!'

We went on to the next Euro round, at Schleiz in eastern Germany. This was our fifth race meeting on that bike, but only our first with that new Grand Prix engine in it. That was pretty daunting because everybody had us down to win this race. Schleiz was a road circuit, and they had me tagged as a roads specialist by now. It was 4 miles long, I'd never seen the place before, and to cap it all it *pissed* it down, all the time we were there, and I mean proper torrential rain. I'd never ridden this bike in the wet before, so I was crapping myself. I was sitting there on this fourteen grand engine, with a ten grand chassis underneath me, and off we went on a wing and a prayer! But we qualified in pole position again, we were bloody quickest, I really couldn't believe it. When we went out in the race itself, again it was pouring with rain. I was kind of confident after our performance in practice, but it was still good competition that I was up against. There were thirty-five bikes on the grid and I'd say the top ten were all really good guys, but even so we won it by 17 seconds! Off we went, and it was unbelievable. There was a 160 mile an hour straight down the back of that circuit with Armco barrier either side of it, and the bike was aquaplaning down the entire length of it. It was wheel-spinning in top gear, at 160 miles an hour, it was truly awesome! We got taken up on to the podium after we had won, and it was really special because the garlands in Germany are just outstanding. They are great big things covered in gold leaf, with German flags of red, black and yellow around them, really spectacular looking. It made me feel like a Formula One racing car hero back in the sixties! When you've won a race it makes it all the more special when they make a big do of it like that, and I sometimes wish the TT organizers would take a leaf out of the German book in that respect! It was a great atmosphere, the whole event was just amazing, and while we were on the podium the organizer of the meeting came up to me. He handed me the winnings, which was about £1,000 in German marks. This guy was also involved in the World Championships, and while he was shaking my hand, he asked would I like a wild card ride at the Czech Grand Prix next weekend. I said, 'Mate, you won't have to ask me twice, I'll be there!' A wild card entry meant that you would get a ride at the event, but you wouldn't get start money or prize money, just the privilege of being invited. And it *was* a privilege because the World Championships then were outstanding. There was Steve Webster,[16] Rolf Biland, great names all of them, people like Darren Dixon the defending World Champion, there was Steve Abbott, Paul Güdel, there was literally a list of Grand Prix winners, and I thought, 'I'm there!' It was just a brilliant feeling.

After we got off the podium, I remember telling Peter, 'That was unbelievable!' He said to me, 'Yeah, it was brilliant, so are we going to Czecho?' I answered without hesitating, 'You bet we are!' We got back to our awning, all our team were there, my mate Billy Quayle, my brother Graham, Norman Burgess, Mike Clark, all of the lads, and they were already drinking beer. I walked in and said, 'Lads, if anyone wants to go home tonight they're going to have to hitch a ride cos we're going to CZECHO!!' A big roar went up, and none of them went home. We celebrated with about 30,000 gallons of lager that night. The whole paddock had a really good crack, and it was a fantastic atmosphere there. This sounds really bad and selfish – probably because it was – but none of us had mobile phones back then, and not one of us thought to go and find a pay-phone to ring up and tell someone at home that we weren't coming back. We just took off. We spent three days in convoy with Stuart Muldoon's team and Steve Abbott's team, going to the Czech Republic. On the way we had a couple of pretty wild nights in Prague partying – all lads' stuff! – but eventually we got to the Brno circuit where the meeting was taking place.

In the first qualifying session for the Czech Grand Prix the gearbox on our bike disintegrated, actually 'exploded' would be a more accurate description. My brother Graham spent probably the next twelve hours, all through the night, rebuilding this gearbox. We had a box of spares and we didn't really know what was in it – it just came with the engine – and using that he put this gearbox back together. It was an amazing job that he did, and it was enough to get us qualified. We made it into the arse end of qualifying, just! We went out for the race, on the warm-up lap the heavens opened, and it came down with torrential rain again. So they gave us five minutes to decide what tyres to put on. We went for wet-weather tyres, and sitting on the grid waiting for the start, Peter leant over the fairing to me and said, 'Dave, do you think we've made the right choice, because apparently it dries up really quick here when it does stop raining?' I replied, 'Well, from where I'm sitting, that guy at the front, Rolf Biland, he's got a set of treads on, and if they're good enough for him they're good enough for me!' There were only three bikes in the race that put treaded tyres on. The rest had a combination of slicks and cut slicks, or cut slicks and wets. So off we went and we were seventeenth on the grid at the start of that race. We were ninth at the end of the first lap and by the sixth lap we were up to sixth place. We diced with Paul and Charly Güdel, and they were in a tussle with Darren Dixon for the world title at that point. Güdel actually cut across me when I tried to pass him. I was a bit of a pussy really, because I was still a little overawed at being there in the first place. Everybody knew who I was because of my TT results and Euro results, and I think they thought, 'We can't have this bastard coming here trying to mix it with us!' I remember going up alongside Charly Güdel and looking at him as though to say, get your finger out, get a move on! I spent about three laps wasting my time on this, and it cost us a lot better result, but eventually he got sick of me coming up alongside and cut across and smashed into my fairing. Well, that was it. I thought, 'I'm not having any of that, I don't care who you are or what you're trying to win!' He had the wrong tyres on, and I had the right tyres on, so my first serious attempt at passing him stuck, and off we went. We got up to sixth place and crossed the line with Steve Abbott half a bike's length ahead of us. It was a really special day. We'd come from the TT to the European Championship round at Schleiz, which was the hardest circuit in Europe in lots of ways, won there, the first time on the bike in wet weather, and then gone on to our first Grand Prix. It was an amazing run. We got some more good results later that year, at Donington and Silverstone. We were fourth at Silverstone. At Donington we were leading by a country mile when the ignition failed, so we lost out in the race but we'd qualified in pole position for that one as well. We went down to Spain, to Catalonia for the last ride of the year. We finished twelfth there, which was still a decent result at world level, but we were really running out of money by this stage. I think the twenty grand I'd set out with had dwindled to about two hundred quid by that event, and we just weren't putting the spares into the engine that we should have been.

There was a lot of travelling that 1996 European season, but we bought a Bedford truck, a great big old turbo-charged horse transporter, and converted the back of it. We took all the gear out of it, and the doors and all the stuff for the horses, and turned it into a mobile race workshop. One funny aspect of that season was that we were so skint that we could really hardly afford to go to these long-haul destinations. We certainly couldn't afford to do it on pump diesel, so we found a way round it: we used to carry four 45-gallon drums in the back of the truck. We filled them with red diesel – agricultural diesel – from a farm in Lancashire, because it was only £1 a gallon! So we had these drums all linked up with pipes and another pipe leading to the fuel tank in the truck. We then had it all covered up with plywood like it was a big old tool chest, but when we were crossing one of the European borders the guards figured us out; they banged this with a big stick and caught us out. The guards said, 'No, you go back, you go back, it's a bomb!' so they turned us around and we had to go about another 400 miles to find another border crossing where we could get across. I suppose we were lucky really, as they could have locked us up, but those four drums of red diesel were the only way we could afford to get to some of these places like Germany and the Czech Republic, which were 1,000 miles each way. We also put some nice comfortable living space in the back of this truck and fitted it out to sleep seven. We always took as many people away with us as we could in those days, to split costs and things like that. For all this posh interior, we never thought to put a toilet in the back of it! When we got across the Channel to Calais, the first thing we did when we came off the ferry was go to EastEnders, the hypermarket there, and buy about a thousand bottles of lager. Then we headed off to wherever we were going – usually about three days' travel – and we were all busy drinking this lager. Well, of course, if you drink lager you need to piss all the time, so whoever was driving got fed up with us stopping every five minutes to find a toilet. After a while, Norman Burgess came up with this idea of fitting a funnel with a pipe out of the back of the truck, so that we wouldn't have to stop for any more toilet breaks. Every time someone took a piss out of the back of the truck, we all looked out of the window and there would be a stream of cars behind us with their windscreen wipers going! So as well as the four 45-gallon drums we now had this posh toilet rigged up in the back! But it meant at least we could get on our way without stopping. We went from meeting to meeting in that, a bit like gypsies really!

With the good run that I had in Europe in 1996, I decided that I wouldn't do the TT the following year. I thought that I would try to make a determined effort at Grand Prix racing, and just compete in the World Championship events in 1997. This meant going abroad a lot, and so I needed to be based in England in order to do it properly. I gave up my business on the Isle of Man, pretty much gave up everything, and moved off the Island. The sidecar constructing business was only just getting going then anyway, so that didn't matter too much. My main earner, though, was my car bodywork business, which I had set up in 1990 in a garage in Kelly Brothers' yard in Kirk Michael. My brother was working for me, I was doing car bodywork repairs, servicing, that kind of thing, but I couldn't keep that going while I was away. I'm not a good enough businessman for that! So I just thought, 'Give it up.' My heart was set on chasing a World Championship dream, and I left to do that, but ultimately it didn't work out. The whole venture, sadly, was way underfunded, and I just didn't have the budget to see it through. I lost a couple of what were promised as big sponsors, who just didn't materialize. I still tried, but halfway through the season I had to pull out. It was a struggle work-wise as well in England, so in the end I moved back to the Isle of Man. We did have two good results in the 1997 World Championship season, in the first two rounds at the Hungaroring in Hungary where the Formula One car races are held, and the A1 Ring in Austria. We got a sixth and a seventh in those first two rounds, which was good because Rolf Biland, Steve Webster, Darren Dixon, all of those guys were doing it. The machine we used was the one we had used for European Championship races in 1996. All we had done to it since the previous year was repaint the bodywork. The third round was at Assen, where the bike seized when we were lying fifth or sixth and I came away from there so skint that I thought I just can't carry this on – all the money was getting spent and none was coming in. But it was a good paddock, there was a lot of camaraderie there. That was a paddock where you could go and borrow anything off anybody. If you needed petrol you could get it, everybody used the same things, it was almost like a one-make series, give or take a couple of bikes. If you were that skint that you needed a second-hand tyre, you could get a used tyre just like that, so it was good.

While I was away that year I rented a garage in Garstang, Lancashire from Frank Rathall, who is one of the best two-stroke tuners in the world. He did a bit of work for me on sidecar engines over the years, but one day I was in there and Joey Dunlop turned up in this plain white van, with the bike that he was going to be using in 1997, a brand-new RS250 Honda that he had just been supplied with. He wanted Frank to tune it and so they put it on the dyno first and it had something like 80.5 brake horsepower. Frank said, 'It's pretty good that, Joey.' Joey with his broad Ulster accent said, 'Yes, but it'll be even better when you've tickled it, Frank.' Well, they spent a week on it, tried different exhausts on it, all sorts of things, and it gained half a horsepower! They were gutted, but Joey still went out and won on it! It just goes to show that people set a lot of store by tuning and other gimmicks but usually it's raw talent on its own that wins races, rather than anything else.

When I returned to live on the Isle of Man again, within a month of coming back, Tommy Leonard (who was the main Honda dealer on the Island) rang me. Tommy told me that the following year, 1998, was Honda's fiftieth anniversary and they were looking to get as many top riders out on their bikes at the TT as possible. Honda really wanted to win everything, every class at the TT that year, and in the end I think they more or less did. Tommy set up a meeting between me and Bob McMillan, who was then the general manager of the motorcycle division of Honda UK. I met with him over breakfast at Admiral House, a top hotel on Douglas Promenade, and he just said, 'Right, tell me what you want!' I told him. The only thing I was scared to ask for was money, and I didn't! I didn't ask for a ha'penny in wages, but they supplied me with two fantastic engines, and a spares budget to look after them. So that teamed me up with Mick Boddice as the two official Honda Britain sidecar drivers, both of us riding in Honda colours! Boddice was a bit of a different story; he had grown up in a paddock where a lot of the people he had raced with as a young man had now retired from competing, and had got themselves good jobs, people like Neil Tuxworth with Honda for instance. With these connections he had made, he got himself some Honda UK support early on in the 1990s, and he stayed with them more or less throughout that decade. We both had full technical backup from Honda, whatever we needed. It was a great set-up.

So we went into the 1998 TT for the first time as part of the Honda Britain team. The funny thing was, in the practice session on the Wednesday night we broke down out on the course, at Sulby Bridge, but we managed to get going again and get back to the pits. While this was going on, there had been a miscommunication between Sulby Bridge and the Grandstand. The marshals had rung to say that I was making adjustments and was heading off again, but that message never got through, so my brother headed off in the van along all the bloody back roads to pick me up. So there we were waiting for him back at the Grandstand, sat outside the Hailwood Centre, having a cup of tea, just sat on the bike talking crap really, when a top rider, one of my rivals, walked up, with a smug look on his fucking mouth and he said, 'Well, I bet you wish you'd never chosen to ride a Honda, because you'll not win on it, Dave!' and he must have been maybe the tenth person, or maybe I'd had a dozen people say that to me that week, and I just thought, 'You small-minded wanker, just because you can't accept that you've got past it, you're taking pleasure in the thought that I can't win on this thing!' As these things tend to do with me, that just made me all the more determined to succeed. We'd had a troubled practice week, I'd have to admit that. I had Dougie Jewell in the chair with me, and he was struggling with it, he wasn't happy at all on the bike. But on Thursday afternoon practice we went out and I set the fastest lap of the week, we lapped at over 110 miles an hour. And all of a sudden, the whole attitude of the paddock changed towards Dave picking this disastrous Honda engine that wouldn't win!

The first sidecar race in that year's TT was cancelled due to the weather, and I got misquoted to holy hell in the *MotorCycle News* as a result. Somebody, a journalist, rang me up the day before the second race, Race B, was due to be run and asked me what I thought about it all. He said, 'So Dave, what are your feelings about the cancellation of the first race?' and I replied, 'Well, we can't do anything about it, it's pissed down with rain for four or five days, it can't be helped.' Then he said, 'Yeah, but you've got to be happy that they have put all the prize money from Race A on to Race B, making what is effectively the biggest prize fund ever for a single race in the sidecar event.' So I answered, 'Well, I'm not going to tell you that I'm unhappy when I stand a very good chance of winning it.' Then he said, 'Yeah, but don't you think it's unfair to the people down the other end of the grid?' And, getting exasperated with the whole conversation by now, I said, 'Well, no, I don't think it's unfair to those people, simply because they were never going to be in a position to win that money anyhow.' That's still my feeling today, and would be for ever, because it's the truth! It's a prize fund, and a prize fund is to be won. Not evenly distributed! He really pissed me off, because the way he asked it was as if it was my fault that it was all done that way! But he kept on with it, saying it was unfair, and I said, 'No, it isn't unfair. We've got a lot of guys out there in that paddock that have come here for a holiday, let's face it.' So what he printed in *MotorCycle News* was that I wasn't prepared to share a prize fund with a bunch of six-lap holiday racers! Well, half the grid wanted to lynch me after that one. I had serious threats, abusive threats after that. The jealousy was unbelievable. They all thought I was getting tens of thousands of pounds to 'ride for Honda'. What a load of crap! In fact a lot of them actually thought I'd bought my house with what I'd been paid by Honda. I bought my first house in October 1998, and because of the timing of it, the word went round that I'd bought it with the money I got from them – this shitty little dump hole in Regaby with a flat roof that was leaking, and windows falling out!

The race itself wasn't a great event, for a variety of reasons. I'd still got passenger issues (Dougie was really uncomfortable on the bike and had actually told me at one point during practice that he wanted off the thing). So I had to ride with this in mind. I had to ride with a guy who didn't really want to be there. As bad luck would have it, the weather was atrocious. At the beginning of the race it was damp in some places, properly wet in others; there were leaves *everywhere*. I went off the start line, and I wouldn't say that my heart wasn't totally in it, but I was just so apprehensive going out to ride, because of both the weather conditions and Dougie's insecurities on the bike. So I set about the race as best I could – but you can get an idea of how uncharacteristic it was for me from the fact that at the Hawthorn Rob Fisher, who set off at number 2, passed me – not in the real world would that ever happen! I'd set the quickest lap of practice, only several seconds short of the lap record, and Rob just wasn't on that kind of pace that year. He was on a mission now, though, but I just thought, 'I've got to ride this race using my bloody head.' I knew the bike would finish, that went without saying. Even so, I had to think carefully how I treated this race, because I could either get a fist in my back, saying, 'I don't want to go round any more, Dave', or I could go sideways into a bloody hedge because of the conditions. So I had a lot going on in my head, and that's without half the paddock wanting to put me up on a shooting range into the bargain!

Off I went, taking it steady, and once Fisher had passed me I just sat on his tail; I sat on his back tyre, and just before Sulby Straight a plume of smoke came out from the underneath of his bike. I thought to myself, 'That's it, boy, you've popped it.' I was third when Fisher went out, and that promoted me up to second, and then it was just a matter of time really, just a case of plugging away. Once I knew Dougie was comfortable with going round how I was riding – and I wasn't getting any indication that he wasn't – we went on and won the race. Yes we won it, and yes we scooped up all that prize money, and yes we won it under Honda colours. But the reality of it was that at the Honda presentation afterwards, when they got all of us winning riders up on stage, the only thing we all had in common was that we rode a bike, because the others, the solo riders, all had a back pocket full of cash. They were all professional riders, and I was basically a privateer with Honda backing. But the other big difference between me and those other boys was that I'd built that bike myself from scratch. Some great engineers had pulled together to build that bike, on and off the Isle of Man. It was built *here*, and not in Japan! All those other boys did was sling a leg over the bike and then tell a mechanic if it was shit or not!

Before the end of that year life dealt me and my family one of those shitty blows which sometimes hit you literally from out of nowhere. In November my youngest brother, Allan, was killed in a road-bike accident. He was only twenty-one years old, and he was just going home after work on this cold and damp evening when he was in collision with a truck and lost his life almost instantly. Like every death in a family, it was a shit time, especially when it's as tragic as that. He was so young, and the poor kid had had a fight all his life. He was born premature, and had the last rites read to him in his cot. He only had partial vision, he had one good eye and one that didn't really work, but he still went on to become a really good bowler for St John's Cricket Club. He never had any aspirations to go racing but he loved following the bikes, and watching them; Carl Fogarty he thought was great, and it was just sad that he had to go like that. He was just starting to live, really, a young man with everything going for him.

For the 1999 TT, Craig Hallam took over from Doug Jewell as my passenger. Doug was brought up on a very different kind of bike, so he had to cope with both my riding style and my machine, which was built with me (and my style) in mind. So he had two new things to cope with there, after many years on another kind of outfit. He was about forty-two years of age then, which was pushing the boundaries for anybody on a sidecar. It's not the easiest thing in the world being a passenger, by any means, I'd be the first to acknowledge that. Anyway, I got Craig on the side, he was young and talented, and a good sidecar driver as well, so he understood what the bike was doing a lot of the time. Between us we could pretty much iron out any problem that was going on with it. It's quite unusual for a passenger to be a driver as well, but that guy was also equally talented on a solo machine. He was a winner at National level on several different makes of motorcycle, so he was an exceptional character and a brave lad. With him as a passenger I knew I could go as hard as I could, there were no worries there. This year, 1999, was another celebration year for Honda – it was their fortieth year of competing at the TT. I built another new bike, with a newer generation Honda engine in it, an FX model. We were quickest by something like 4 miles an hour in practice. We absolutely dominated it. In fact we came to within one and a half seconds of setting the first ever sub-20-minute lap. That, if you stop to think about it, was a pretty amazing thing. That was over ten years ago, and there are guys struggling to do that now. There are only a handful of us who have ever gone under twenty minutes, and in my case back in 1999 that was on an old carburettored bike, with a CDI ignition unit. It was so basic, it had restricted carburettors, everything. My race craft and my whole way of thinking about riding had changed now. I didn't think so much about winning, I just wanted to set the track alight, and be faster than anything else by a long way. I lost races through trying to be fastest, and trying something different. Winning now held less of an appeal for me; it sounds strange, but that had dwindled, although the appeal of riding around the course was still there. I just wanted to push the speed barrier as far as I could, to take it to another level. That did cost me races, I know.

I enjoyed the first leg of the TT that year, it was an excellent race; we won it by a very wide margin. We set a lap record of 112.76mph in that first outing. It was about 2 seconds slower than we'd done in practice, so I was a bit disappointed with *that*, as I would have thought we would have gone quicker, but anyway that was the way it was. The

This is me on the left at Glen Maye in 1965, I was aged two. Already I had three-wheelers on the brain. *(Molyneux Collection)*

Myself and brother Kevin in 1967. I've now added a fuel tank to my machine. I'm not sure if it would pass scrutineering though! *(Molyneux Collection)*

Outside Tower House, our family home in Kirk Michael, 1972. Left to right: me, my sister Judy, my sister Georgina and my brother Kevin. *(Molyneux Collection)*

My father John Molyneux's FIM competition licence from 1977. He was my inspiration and the reason for my love of sidecars. *(Molyneux Collection)*

Howard Oates (right) and me with George O'Dell, in 1977. The photo was taken on Ballamoda Straight where O'Dell and Kenny Arthur were testing. Kenny took the photo for me. *(Molyneux Collection)*

John Molyneux and George Oates awaiting the start in the 1977 Sidecar A TT. They finished 7th; O'Dell won the race. *(Molyneux Collection)*

Molyneux and Oates in their final race, at the 1977 Ulster Grand Prix. Moments after this photograph was taken, the pair crashed, killing Oates instantly and leaving my father fighting for his life. *(Molyneux Collection)*

George O'Dell at the Palace Lido, Douglas in 1977. Sidecar World Champion George had come over with his outfit to raise money for the Oates and Molyneux Children's Fund. *(Molyneux Collection)*

Just before my first sidecar race, at Jurby airfield, Isle of Man, April 1980. Paul Craine (Sid) was in the chair. We finished third! *(Molyneux Collection)*

My first attempt at the TT, 1985. I had to beg to get into the event, and when I was finally allowed to compete I went out as number 93, last outfit away. *(Molyneux Collection)*

Myself and Paul Kneale (centre) after our double win at the 1986 Southern 100 races. My future passenger Colin Hardman is on the right. *(Molyneux Collection)*

With Alan Langton at Donington Park in 1988, aboard a Padgetts Yamaha machine. We were there for the British Championship round. *(Courtesy of Eric Whitehead)*

With Colin Hardman aboard the Bregazzi Yamaha, during the 1989 TT. This was the year we took our first win. *(Molyneux Collection)*

Celebrating after our first TT win; Race A at the 1989 event. Left to right: sponsor Frank Higley, myself, Eric Bregazzi, Colin Hardman and Daphne Higley. Without the help of the Bregazzis and others I would never have achieved this win. *(Molyneux Collection)*

Riding with Karl Ellison at the 1991 TT. Note the backpack that I'm wearing here – I was filming an on-board lap for a TT video. *(Molyneux Collection)*

Competing in the 1993 TT. That year Karl and I really cleaned up, by winning both races! *(Courtesy of Eric Whitehead)*

At Quarterbridge in the 1994 TT. We had a real challenge on our hands that year in the form of Rob Fisher. *(Molyneux Collection)*

Myself and Peter Hill, at Donington Park for the 1994 British Sidecar Championship. We finished second in this event. *(Molyneux Collection)*

Myself and brother Graham in our film debut. (Detail from *Cremaster 4*: The Isle of Man, 1994. *Copyright Matthew Barney / Courtesy Gladstone Gallery, New York)*

In pole position for the Dutch round of the European Championship, at Assen in March 1995. People there were laughing at our machine, but they soon stopped! *(Molyneux Collection)*

In action at the 1995 Ulster Grand Prix. We won, but that was the only time that I ever competed at this event. *(Courtesy of Eric Whitehead)*

Racing in the Czech Republic at the Most circuit, 1995. It was a European Championship round, and the heat there was incredible. *(Courtesy of František Feigl)*

On the podium after victory in the Sidecar B race, 1996 TT. We took that TT to a different level. *(Molyneux collection)*

Waiting for the start at Schleiz. This was the German round of the 1996 European Championships. We were in pole position. *(Courtesy of Dieter Fleischer)*

Racing in the wet at Schleiz, 1996. We won the round here, in spite of the conditions. *(Courtesy of Dieter Fleischer)*

August 1996: winners at the European Championship round at Schleiz, Germany. The Germans made you feel like a 60s Formula One winner with their gold-coloured garlands. *(Courtesy of Dieter Fleischer)*

Racing in the 1996 Czech Grand Prix at Brno. We were handed a wildcard entry for this event, and finished 6th in our first ever Grand Prix! *(Molyneux Collection)*

The machine in Honda Britain colours for the 1998 TT. I had Doug Jewell in the chair this year. *(Courtesy of Eric Whitehead)*

Looking pleased after victory in the 1998 Sidecar TT. There was only one sidecar race that year, with double prize money; I scooped it. *(Molyneux Collection)*

SIDECAR

Myself and Craig Hallam testing at Jurby airfield before the 1999 TT. I knew I could go as fast as it was possible with Craig on board; he was a brave lad. *(Molyneux Collection)*

In action during the Sidecar World Cup, 2000; this photo was taken at Hockenheim during the German round, where we finished 5th. *(Courtesy of Roger Lohrer)*

2002 at the TT and back with Colin Hardman in the chair. Colin injured himself quite badly on the morning of the first race. *(Molyneux Collection)*

In action in Honda colours during the 2002 TT. It was a testament to Colin's strength of character that we got round at all. *(Courtesy of Eric Whitehead)*

A classic TT image: coming down off the mountain at Creg-ny-Baa, 2004. We change down to second gear at this point, going down from 150mph to take the corner at 70mph. *(Courtesy of Dave Collister)*

2006: In practice for the TT. In the Thursday night session we flipped the machine at Rhencullen. *(Courtesy of Trevor Burgess)*

On the final lap, 1 June 2006. Here we are at the end of Cronk Y Voddy; moments after this photo was taken we were approaching Rhencullen. *(Courtesy of Dave Collister)*

The 2006 crash: the aftermath. This photo shows the machine after it had caught fire in the smash at Rhencullen. *(Courtesy of Alwyn Collister)*

In practice for the 2007 Centenary TT. This machine was an almost exact replica of that which had been destroyed the previous year, apart from the engine; it just couldn't match the speed of that bike. *(Courtesy of Dave Collister)*

Myself and Kenny Arthur, following the 2007 TT parade lap. Kenny passengered my hero George O'Dell in 1977. Behind is the replica of the O'Dell machine, which I built to ride in the parade lap. *(Courtesy of Dave Collister)*

With Terry Windle at the 2007 TT. Terry built the original outfit that George O'Dell had ridden in 1977. *(Molyneux Collection)*

In the colours of Peter Lloyd Racing for the 2007 Superside series. After my crash the previous year, I still wasn't fit enough to give this campaign 100 per cent. *(Molyneux Collection)*

The machine in Suzuki colours for the 2008 TT. This is Race B in which we finished second. *(Courtesy of Dave Collister)*

Dan Sayle and myself, Suzuki-powered again at the 2009 TT. We took victory in Race A that year. *(Courtesy of Dave Collister)*

Myself and passenger Patrick Farrance in the 2010 TT. We raced in the green and black colours of Kawasaki. *(Courtesy of Dave Collister)*

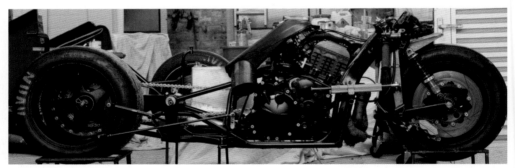

The 2010 machine stripped down to the chassis. The powerful Kawasaki engine is clearly visible here. *(Courtesy of John Caley)*

second race came and the oil filter housing split on the last lap of the event going down towards Handley's Corner, spraying oil up all over us. That was the end of that. I had thought that the engine had blown up; it wasn't until we got home that we discovered what the problem was. Anyway, it wouldn't have changed the result, we couldn't have fixed it at the side of the road. But we were in a 2-minute lead at that time, on the last lap of a TT, cake-walking it. So it was disappointing that we broke down when we really had that race in the bag. Also I was a bit aggrieved that as a result we didn't get to go under the 20-minute barrier as I had hoped, and that then became my new goal, because we had found in practice that, 'Jesus, it's achievable.' We nearly got it that night, and we were almost there. But we didn't get it then, and for various reasons it didn't happen for a number of years afterwards.

During the TT in 1999, Honda held a special dinner at Admiral House for all of their riders past and present, or as many who could make it to the Isle of Man anyway. I think there were about forty of them there; people like Luigi Taveri, Ron Haslam and Jim Redman. I was sat alongside Joey Dunlop; he was a hell of a guy. Up to that point we'd only probably said about half a dozen words to each other in the paddock; we'd always acknowledged each other, but that was all. Anyway, at this particular dinner he leaned over to me and sort of whispered to me in his Northern Ireland accent, 'Fucking hell, you're crazy, you are!' I said, 'What are you talking about?' and he told me this story. He said, 'I was broke down yesterday at Rhencullen, and I was sat on the hedge there, near the end of the session and I heard this fucking bike coming,' (that was just how he spoke). He said, 'I heard this fucking bike coming and the throttle was just pinned open, so I leaned back and shouted over to the marshals, "Someone's going to bloody crash here, they're not shutting off!" and the marshals shouted back, "Don't worry, it'll be Molyneux!"' He was shaking his head and he found this really amusing. It's really nice and flattering when people like him come out with something like that! They actually sit up and notice you, but David Jefferies was the same, we used to have a bit of banter, he used to call me every loony under the sun! My main rival at this time, though, was Rob Fisher. Really, from 1993, when he first came on the scene, he was fast. He was an instant success. In 1994 he had won two races, and so it went on. Between then and 2002 realistically it was always going to be Rob Fisher or myself who won at the Isle of Man Sidecar TT. It's a satisfying thought, though, that he won in 1995 and 2002 riding one of my bikes! At the end of 1998 Mick Boddice had retired from racing, and Rob got the other Honda ride. It was like a backup plan for them. They knew if I failed, which did happen on several occasions, Fisher was there to pick up the pieces. Likewise, if he failed I was there. We were very close in ability, I think, but it was a question of who could outfox who, and who had the best bike.

In 2000 Honda were great, they supported me in another World Championship attempt. I also had some terrific local support from Peter and Lorraine Tyer, hoteliers from Merseyside who had retired to the Isle of Man. Peter had introduced himself to me in 1998, he was very into motorbikes, in a big way, and it was he and Lorraine through the Suites Hotel in Knowsley who put together a big financial package to support me, alongside Honda. The series was now run with World Superbikes, not with Grands Prix. This I thought was good, because it was a nice fresh new beginning. It was now called the Sidecar World Cup, and was run on some fantastic circuits all over the world. It was a completely different riding style, and a different approach was needed, because the bikes were totally different to TT machines. They put four-stroke engines in the class, and we chose a Honda Blackbird engine, as we were being supported by Honda. But it turned out just not to be a very good tool. It didn't like being tuned; when you tuned it, it blew up. We had endless engine failures; engine blow-ups one after another, and it just didn't work out. In the end we figured out that the problem was with the crankshaft, which was too powerful and kept flexing within the engine. We tried reinforcing it with steel plates, but even that wasn't enough. That was just the way it went. To keep the machine reliable, we resorted to using an ordinary road-bike engine, which we got from a breaker's yard. When we got it, it was covered in oil and crap but we got it cleaned up and slotted it in. We rode on some fabulous circuits around the world during that series; we went to Kyalami in South Africa, that was the first round. We flew out to South Africa, and the bike went out air freight. We stayed at a lodge called Ulusaba, it was pretty ritzy, a really nice place! A sponsor called John Dyer covered our costs for the whole team to stay there, he's from South Africa and has Isle of Man connections, and he was good enough to put us all up. Racing out there was fantastic, the weather was good of course, but the chance to race at a track like Kyalami was pretty special. It's a Formula One car circuit and when they race at a circuit it's usually a good track. It carries a bit of history with it as well, and if you've got racing in your head and in your heart, to go to places like that is an amazing feeling. When you think that Ayrton Senna and people like him have raced on the same patch of tarmac as you, that's great!

The bike was then air-freighted out from there to Phillip Island, in Australia. We were there when Carl Fogarty had the accident which effectively ended his racing career. I was standing at the end of the pit lane when it came up on the TV screens that he'd had this accident, and the whole paddock went dead – it was a scary moment. People did fear the worst because for a short time there was just no word coming back as to what had gone wrong. I seem to remember they got him back to the medical centre in the paddock, and then they airlifted him away. Phillip Island itself wasn't anything to get excited about. We stayed in a bed and breakfast in a place called Victoria, and commuted back and forth to the circuit. Then everything was air-freighted back and we set about the European scene, so we rode in Germany, Holland, Italy, Spain and England. I was racing against Steve Webster, Klaus Klaffenböck,[17] guys like that. They were the men to beat. Our best result of the year was a fifth place at Hockenheim in Germany, which is the fastest circuit in Europe. Strangely enough, Hockenheim resembles many parts of the Isle of Man TT mountain circuit. The old layout of the course, which went right out round the back into the woodlands, was surrounded by Armco barrier for a start, so there was nowhere to run off if you overcooked it. It was over 3 miles long. The straight was nearly a mile long, with a small chicane in the middle of it, which was fast as hell. If you crashed on that outer section round the back of the circuit you were more likely to hit a tree or something than you were not to! There have been some horrendous accidents at Hockenheim, and that's why it's not like that any more. Our bike was clocked through the speed trap there at 176 miles an hour, and it was still nearly 10 miles an hour down on the best bike in that race. If you think about the speeds at the TT, around 145 miles an hour, it just shows how fast those bikes were. The main difference with the TT was the road surface. On a track like Hockenheim it's a flat surface. There is no camber in the middle of the road for the water to run off. On a short circuit the gutter is usually on the inside or outside of the track. It's a billiard table compared with the TT circuit, which is very rough in places and very hard on the machinery.

We were competitive there with a bike that was almost 40 horsepower down on power compared with the other bikes in the race. I was really satisfied with that, because it was like winning a B race in a way. In effect we were the best of the rest! Klaffenböck and Hauzenberger were team mates, and so were Steinhausen and Webster, both pairs on identical bikes, and they had had no expense spared whatsoever. Those bikes were the ultimate World Championship machines. They were all using Suzuki engines, all of them, that was the best engine to use in that class, but I could hardly use that engine with Honda written down the side of the bike! Having Honda sponsorship was a double–edged sword in a way, because the Blackbird engine just wasn't up to it. To give Honda their due, it was never intended to be. It wasn't built as a race engine, it was a touring bike engine. Entering this series was something I wanted to try, and

Honda were good enough to support me on it and try it with me. To be fair to them, a manufacturer is really sticking its neck on the line when they put an engine into a sidecar, because it has twice the work to do. The only way we could have extracted more power from that engine would have been to spend long tens of thousands of pounds on it, using specialist-made aftermarket parts, and there was no way that was going to happen. The nearest engine to that was the Honda Fireblade, which was only 900cc, making it 300cc smaller than the Suzuki, so that was never an option to try either.

We had a few thrills and spills along the way in that series. I was on for my best ever result at a world event on the last lap at Assen in Holland. I was lying fourth, and the guy in front of me seized his bike up directly in my path. I had to take avoiding action, and we both crashed into the gravel. So there I went, four corners from getting a podium position at a World Championship round and I ended up on my ear! We weren't badly hurt, but the bike was upside down, and we couldn't restart. My passenger there was Lee Aubrey, a Welsh lad. Peter Hill, who had first ridden with me in 1993, joined me as passenger for the early rounds of the World Cup. Because I was doing that series I didn't do the TT in 2000. We were right at the top of our game yet again at the TT, and again I had decided instead to go off chasing this bloody World Championship dream, which just didn't work out for us. I couldn't afford to do both events, and I wasn't earning a living from the World Championship, so I was definitely worse off financially chasing this bloody dream than I would have been if I'd simply stayed at home, just doing the TT and fixing bent cars! Still, I know I would have regretted not doing it. I gave it a go, and unless you do that you are never going to find out what really is possible. I was fast, I was competitive, but things just didn't work out.

In 2001 I was planning to compete in the TT again. I had a good sponsor lined up in the form of a South African friend who lived on the Isle of Man, but the event was cancelled due to the outbreak of foot and mouth disease in the UK. The authorities in the Isle of Man were worried that people who had been in contact with the disease in England might well be going on to farmland as spectators at the TT, and that was a risk they just didn't want to take. The whole event was scrapped, for the first time since the war. In some ways the break was good, for both me personally and for Honda. I'd built a new bike, which used Honda's first ever 600cc injection engine, and it has to be said it was not good. In sidecar trim it was pretty poor. The electronics package which came with it was in its most primitive state. It would only allow you to increase the fuelling to the engine by 30 per cent, so it didn't have anything like enough fuel going into the thing. As time went on, later that year, you could buy various smaller add-on aftermarket parts which allowed you to get that up to 100 per cent, and get the machine to run better. With a sidecar, you have to remove the standard equipment which comes with the engine, like the airbox, and you have to change the fuel map, in order to get more fuel through, and this engine basically wouldn't allow us to do that. It was so dog slow that it was embarrassing. If we had gone out to do the TT with that engine it would have been a disaster. During that year I only rode the bike two or three times. The first time convinced me that this injection system was never going to work. After that, we converted back to our system of carburettors and CDI ignition. It went well then, but if the TT had actually been on we would not have got into it anyway. We would have run out of time, as it was so late in the year that we finally got some sort of decent performance out of that engine. Looking at it that way, it was a good thing that the TT didn't go ahead in 2001.

In other ways it was a very bad year for me. At that time I was dependent on two main sources of income. One was building bikes, and the other was competing at the TT as a professional rider. The TT didn't run, so I got no pay-day from that (though I probably wouldn't have done so even if it had, given the state of the engine). Also I had five provisional orders from riders for bikes leading up to that TT, and all but one of those riders cancelled their order, because they thought that with no TT they could last another year without a new bike. So I effectively lost a year's work. Again, I was misquoted in the newspapers. I remember that a reporter rang me up and asked me what effect the cancellation would have on me, given that I built bikes for a living and also raced them for a living. I said, 'Well, I've lost a year's wage, effectively.' There was no point in feeling sorry for myself, it had happened and that's all there was to say. But the way some of the newspapers on the Isle of Man presented it was as if I was a whingeing arsehole, feeling sorry for himself and feeling hard done by. It wasn't the first time I've been misquoted in my life, and probably won't be the last, in fact I often think 'misquote' should be my middle name! But there's no getting away from the fact that it was a bloody lean year, and financially I was right on the edge. At one point I really feared that I would lose my house, but I got by on welding cars, doing some spraying, bodywork, that kind of thing.

In 2002 I got Colin Hardman back on as my passenger. Over the years we hadn't raced together I think Colin had had some matters in his personal life that he needed to sort out. I know that he also had big problems holding his job down while he was racing. His employers did not like him doing it one little bit. But since he had been out of it I think he realized how much he had missed racing, and now he'd sorted some of those other problems out as well, so he was keen to get back into it. Age wasn't really a big issue to Colin during the 1990s. He was still a fit man, absolutely teetotal, fit as a fiddle, and he always looked after himself. I bumped into him on Strand Street in Douglas one day, and he asked who was passengering for me that year in the TT. I answered that I didn't know at the minute. He offered straight away, and I thought, 'Well, what the hell.' He'd kept himself fit, and I needed a passenger, so we got back together. Unfortunately in that 2002 event he was commuting on his road bike from Douglas where he lived, up to Regaby where I lived, and had a road traffic accident on the way. I was waiting for him in my garage, wondering where the hell he was, when I got a phone call, and someone told me that Colin had had this accident. This was four hours before the start of the first race. He'd been checked over at the roadside, convinced the medics he was alright, and got himself up to the Grandstand, because he didn't want to let me down or himself down. There at the paddock he met me, with an arsy attitude towards him. I was a bit unsympathetic at that particular moment, I know. But at the same time I'd just spent the last seven months building a bike to do a job, with Honda behind me, and tens of thousands of pounds of sponsorship having gone into that effort. I couldn't just get anybody to ride that bike with me. It was either game over or Colin got on. How he managed this I don't know, but he somehow wriggled out of getting a medical before the race. As we waited in the paddock I said to him, 'If you can't do this, just do not do it.' I was angry with him at the time, angry that he'd chosen to ride his road bike, instead of just using his car like he had done all that week. I ranted at him, 'Of all the days you could choose to ride your bloody road bike, you chose today, Colin.' He'd obviously hurt himself. I'd seen him in pain before, and he could carry pain that man, carry it with the best of them, but his right hand was badly swollen, and he'd really knocked himself about. But he convinced me that he was fine to ride, and he got on the bike, so we went out and raced. We finished fourth, and I was seriously hacked off with that result, but for me or anyone else to have expected any more of him would have been ridiculous. He'd had a really bad hiding. I knew straight away after we left the start line that he was struggling, and so I had to ride accordingly. We got the thing round, and in a way it was amazing that we even did that. It was a testament to his strength of character that he was able to complete that race; that was Colin all over. I'd seen that before in the crash we had in 1989. He carried injuries then throughout that TT that he had made light of, but this was more serious. Back then in 1989 we had the accident a week before the TT. This time, he had hurt himself on the morning of the day in which we were due to race.

After that fourth-place result Colin went and spent some time recuperating, and a few days later we went out for Race B in the 2002 TT. We finished second in that race. We diced with Rob Fisher, and it was a thrilling dice according to onlookers and spectators. I went out first, Fisher was second behind me, he caught and passed me on the road, but we diced the whole way round. It was a good race, a fair race, and Colin did well to hold on. Directly after the TT that year, the Isle of Man Sports Council got in touch with me and asked if we would carry the Queen's Commonwealth Games baton, Colin and myself, on the sidecar. We carried this baton on the outfit, on the road with a police escort – a police car front and rear like a rolling road closure – and we took that baton from the National Sports Centre in Douglas down to King William's College in Castletown, where the kids all crowded round to see us. It was nice to be asked to be involved in things like that. Likewise it was quite an honour when the Isle of Man Post Office decided to include me on a stamp they were producing to mark the anniversary of the TT. Manx Telecom once put out a special phone card with myself and Colin on, and a fifty-pence coin was also produced at one point with us on the reverse. I must admit I wasn't too bothered about these things at the time, but looking back it's nice, and flattering in a way. It's there for ever, after all, and it's not everyone who gets to appear on a coin or stamp in their own lifetime, or at all.

Colin went to get himself properly checked out after the TT and it turned out he had broken ribs, broken a bone in his hand, and his coccyx was fractured. He only found these injuries when he went to hospital and got X-rays done after the event. It was a tough one, but I said to Colin after he had the X-rays that I felt I couldn't ride to my full ability in the upcoming Southern 100 (which I was desperate to win) with him on as passenger and with him carrying an injury. It wasn't fair on either of us to carry on at that point. So I got Craig Hallam back on, and we won practically everything then for the rest of that season. We won something like nineteen races on the trot. We won the Southern 100, both Scarborough events, the Cock o' the North in July, the Scarborough Gold Cup, all the Celtic Match Races, the Dutch European Championship round at Assen, it was like we couldn't lose. It was a real contrast with the situation in 2001, in as much as we had really got the engine sorted out now. We really had got it to go. Honda supplied the gear – good bits were coming through from them thick and fast now, like race parts that they were updating – and I got Slick Bass tuning the engines again, he really got them going. We set them up on the carburettors, and the older-type ignition that we had in 1999. Together with the chassis I had built, we had a really good package together at that stage.

As usually happened, I sold that bike at the end of the season to offset some of my costs from racing, and I built a new bike in the early part of 2003. I didn't quite manage to get it finished in time for the start of the TT that year; I also had quite a few to build for other people, so my own got shoved to the back of the queue and didn't get completed until the beginning of practice week. We were quickest in practice again, in every session, but we went out in the first race and the rear wheel bearing collapsed. It went going into Parliament Square in Ramsey, but I had felt there was something that wasn't quite right with it early on in the lap, at Kirk Michael. I was losing my brake pedal, and that was down to the movement in the wheel bearings, which moved the brake disc, and pushed the brake pads back, so when I came to brake I had to pump the pedal. That was in the first lap, and we were leading the race when we broke down. We had it sorted out for the second race, but there was a lot of bad weather that day. It started out damp, and there was a lot of to-ing and fro-ing on the start line. The ACU didn't know whether to hold it back any longer or postpone it or whatever, but anyway in the end we went out, on slick tyres. The weather gradually got worse during the race, there was low cloud on the mountain and puddles on the road, but we won by a considerable amount. After the TT, later that summer we went on to win the Southern 100 once again, and that was my last appearance at

that event. I always had a lot of affection for that event because my
father had raced at it, but I felt that as it was my twentieth year there,
and I'd won fifteen races, seven championships, and held the lap
record there on several occasions, it was time to try other things. I felt
it was time to move on, and leave it to someone else.

In 2004 Honda turned to me and told me that they could help us,
but not to the same extent that they had done in other years. So that
year we were given free rein on the colour scheme of the bike.
Honda told us that if we could get an outside backer to be our title
sponsor, and get some cash for it, then go for it. Martin Bullock and
I are good friends, and he asked me how much it would cost for him
to have the machine in his colours of yellow and black. We agreed a
sum of money, and the bike appeared that year in Martin Bullock
Racing (MBR) livery. We still had some Honda support, we received
two engines from them with HRC race kit parts, and the rest of that
effort was financed by ourselves and by local sponsors like Martin.
That year we put together the first ever fuel-injected bike that
actually went well. The engine had had a few years' development by
this time and it had turned into something that was really special. As
a result it was a pretty easy TT for us. We went out and were fastest
in every practice session, and won both races at an absolute canter,
and nothing went wrong apart from the fact that I broke a bone in
my hand! As we were coming through the Waterworks in the first
race the handlebars flicked out of my grip and I felt this bone in the
back of my left hand pop. Luckily it didn't stop me finishing that
race or starting the next one. Craig Hallam had family commitments
that year so he wasn't available, and that was my first year with Dan
Sayle on board. He was still a kid then, and I thought he had
potential, he looked good on a bike; I watched him on a bike and on
DVDs and I could see that he had natural ability. He's a good
passenger, with the right build, naturally gifted and has a feel for
something that's going fast, whether that is a solo or a sidecar. Also

he has an ear for the mechanics of a machine so all in all we gelled pretty quickly.

Honda stepped up a gear once again at the TT in 2005. We didn't do a lot of racing prior to the TT that year, I think we maybe only did a couple of races at Jurby airfield up to that point. We had a troubled practice week that year. We had a lot of problems with the engine management system on the outfit. By the end of practice week I hadn't even qualified. I'd done two laps on the Saturday, but that was untimed, and I still had to put a timed lap in, but the bike kept breaking down. So by the Friday night the pressure was really on, but we went out and did two laps under 20 minutes, the first time that had ever been done. I'd had a lot of earache during the week, people saying the pressure was on, and if we didn't qualify then we wouldn't be able to race, blah blah blah. I just thought, 'Oh, give us a break.' We'd been out on the Saturday night, and did two laps with the bike straight out of the crate. We knew what speed we'd done that night and so did they, but we'd still been getting these jibes thrown at us all week that we wouldn't be on the grid if we didn't get a lap of practice in that Friday night. Well, we got those laps in, and I think it was Chris Kinley, the radio commentator, who came up to us afterwards and said, 'Dave, you've made history, the first ever sub-20-minute laps.' I was pretty cool about it and just said, 'Oh well, at least we've qualified!'

In the first race, the weather was decidedly dodgy, I think it rained at the start of the race, and a few people were pissed off that they decided to run the race at all because of the tyre problems we have over here. But they started the race anyway, off we went, and we broke down at the top of Barregarrow, with the same problems that we'd been enduring through practice. One of the plug cap coils had burned out, and dropped a cylinder. We pulled it over but we were 45 seconds in the lead at that point, which was one of the biggest leads we'd ever had. We were red hot at that time. Nobody was anywhere near us. Our first lap in that race was near 110 miles an hour, and that was from a standing start in damp conditions, in fact it was more than damp, it was actually raining. We had another practice before the next race and we got to the bottom of what this problem was that had been happening throughout the week; part of the engine management system had been tuned too far and kept breaking apart. We corrected that, went out for that practice lap and it went fantastically well. Again it was under 20 minutes. We went out for the second race, and we strung together three laps under 20 minutes each, did the first ever race average under an hour and set a 116 mile an hour lap record. That race went great really, it was a pretty easy win; the only problem we had was that in the last lap coming out of Governor's Dip one of the back wheel bearings collapsed. I heard it crunch – there are three bearings holding the back axle in place and one had collapsed, so the axle went slightly out of true. It gives the impression that you've got a puncture or something, so I had to drive really slowly from then on. I coasted from Governor's Dip to the finish line, but we still averaged under an hour for that race even with that slight snag at the end.

Later that year, the Lieutenant Governor of the Isle of Man, Air Marshal Sir Ian Macfadyen came to the end of his term of office. I didn't know this, but he'd always wanted to have a go on a sidecar before he left the Isle of Man. Someone from the government rang me up and asked would I take him out on the bike, as a kind of retirement present. I said yes, of course I would. So we met him down at Jurby airfield, he got some leathers on and got on the side and we did a few runs up and down the straight there at Jurby. He was a really nice gentleman, he's an ex-fighter pilot so he was used to going fast, and he said afterwards, 'That's really great!' – he was buzzing with excitement by the time we finished! Border Television came down and covered it, and it was on the TV that evening. So that rounded off a pretty successful year for me in terms of personal achievements.

Chapter 4

To the Edge and Back

The bike that I had ridden in the 2004 TT had Honda's first decent fuel-injected engine in it, and gradually we had developed this engine and that bike into a really awesome package. In 2005 we had broken the 20-minute lap barrier at the TT, an ambition that I had been chasing for some six years, and I had no reason to think that in the following year we would not continue to develop it further. I started out in 2006 with Craig Hallam back on board; he felt that he wanted to do it again, and I thought 'Why not?' We went to some short circuit meetings in England in the early part of that year and we really were fast. We won the first two rounds of the British Championship by a street mile, and when we went into the TT that year we were leading the Championship. It's really not an exaggeration to say that at that particular point in time we were in a different league from everyone else. Wet or dry conditions, it made no difference; there were guys there who professed to be wet-weather specialists, but we just blasted past them, in fact Craig said to me at one point, 'This is ridiculous, it's too easy Dave.' So we went into the TT in a strong position, but throughout practice week Craig didn't seem too happy with the handles on the sidecar platform. I had first ridden with Craig seven years earlier, and my own feeling is that by 2006 it could possibly have been that he had met his limit. Again, as with some of my previous passengers, the speeds were getting higher, and he was getting older. It's a fine line, and a passenger has to be *so* dialled into what he's doing. Anyway, on Wednesday evening practice we set a new lap record from a standing start. It was unbelievable, as a standing start is normally giving away anything between 10 and 15 seconds on a flying lap, but we dipped 2 seconds under my previous best time. We went round in 19 minutes 28 seconds, which is outrageous when you think about it. To this day I still don't know how or why that happened, I really don't! It was amazing really. We weren't going to go out for another practice session that week. I felt so comfortable on that bike, it was so bloody fast, and I had so much confidence in Craig that I thought there was absolutely no way we couldn't win on race day, and I wanted to leave things just as they were.

However, Craig felt that he wanted to get one more practice in, so we went out for the Thursday night practice session. Although we'd broken my own lap record the previous night I wasn't going out looking to do it again that evening, I was simply out there to practise my laps. So we set off with all new tyres and chain and brake pads, and by the time you get to Ballacraine, all of that stuff is bedded in, it's well and truly bedded in, and so you can light the thing up a bit, start to go a lot quicker if you feel comfortable, and I'd never felt more comfortable in twenty years of racing round the TT mountain circuit than I did that night. I don't have a great recollection of what happened next that evening, or an understanding of why it happened. We were about halfway out on our first lap going through the top of Rhencullen. We got what seemed to be a tight line on the right-hander at the top of the hill, which was extremely bumpy, but that gave us an exceptionally good line going into the left-hander, running into the jump. There was no wheel spin, no judder, everything seemed fine. Going down through that corner seemed so quick, it was very, very fast, and as it did so the bike seemed to become a little unstable on the front. It was running on just the edge of the front tyre, which meant that the sidecar wheel was in the air. If a sidecar is running with only the edge of its tyre in contact with the road, then it becomes extremely unstable and difficult to control; but there isn't a great deal you can do about that going at 140 miles an hour on a stretch of road which is only 300 yards long! There isn't an awful lot you can do in that time. I knew I hit the jump in a different place from before, and as soon as I did that the front wheel just climbed high. The minute the air got underneath that thing, it just turned it over. I met a guy quite recently – I didn't know him, but he had been a spectator at Rhencullen that night – and he came up to me in a café and told me that what he saw there was the most frightening thing he'd ever seen at the TT. He told me that as far as he was concerned it was amazing that I hadn't been killed in that incident.

Craig told me afterwards that as it started to rise up, he let go of the bike. He wasn't badly hurt in the crash, just bruised and scuffed a bit I think. But now the bike was going down the road upside down and I was trapped underneath it for a good distance; that was until it struck the stone wall halfway down the hill, where we parted company. All impacts are different. I didn't make contact with the wall myself, but it was probably the force of that impact which pushed my shoulder out. I was under the bike for what seemed like only a short time until it hit the wall, but the worst bit was sliding down the road, being fully aware of what was going on and having time to think, 'How the fuck am I going to get away with this?' and I did really have time to think that! You can either let it go or you can fight it, and if I'm sliding down the road on my ass I'll fight it every time! I did in fact manage to break away from it. In that situation there are things you can do for self-preservation – perhaps not in every incident – but when you're just sliding like a bobsleigh down the road, with the outfit on its streamlining and not on its wheels, you can still steer it to a certain extent.

When everything had come to rest I got up, and I looked up to the top of the hill in total disbelief, thinking, 'What the fucking hell happened there?' I was gobsmacked as to how it had happened, as prior to that everything was going great, and had been all through that lap. The bike caught fire almost straight away. It had travelled down the road upside down, which wore the top of the airbox away and then in turn wore the fuel rail in the top of the engine away. The fuel came out into the airbox and sparks from the road set it alight. When the bike eventually stopped sliding and dug in, it went end over end, righted itself and ended up back on its wheels. It had by then been doused in high-octane race fuel, and it ignited straight away. I guess it must have been burning to a degree inside that airbox even as it was sliding down the road with me underneath it, though my injuries were not caused by the fire. I had two laps' worth of race fuel still in that bike, and it just went up like a candle. Carbon fibre burns very easily; with all the resins in it, it isn't exactly fire-retardant!

My first reaction after I had picked myself up was to get out of the track. It was the usual story, we were first on the road and I didn't want to get hit by a following bike. I walked into a nearby garden, and a kind gentleman from the house came out to see if I was OK. I was holding my right arm, thinking, 'Fuck me, something's not right here.' It was 4 inches longer than it should have been for a start, and it didn't feel as if it was connected somehow. I knew as well that I'd taken a heavy smash in the right shoulder because it wasn't there, it was now inside my ribcage. The guy from the house looked as scared as anyone I've ever seen, poor guy, he'd seen the whole thing happen. The marshals must have been shocked at the incident as well, but they reacted amazingly. I take my hat off to the marshals because it's a hell of a job they've got to do, and the concern on their faces after just witnessing a 140 mile an hour crash, and then the machine going on fire, was obvious. I heard one guy shouting, 'Where is he?' They must have thought I'd been fired over a hedge or something, but then they saw me in the garden. I could see the bike was burning fiercely now but I was resigned to the fact that there was nothing I could do about it. Also I was more worried about myself at that stage. Strange things can happen to you – physically and mentally – when you've taken a heavy knock like that. I was determined that nothing like that was going to happen to me, and I just paced up and down. Shock isn't a good thing, it can be a killer, and I didn't want to go into unconsciousness, so I thought, 'Just bloody well keep pacing up and down.' The medics came into the garden and they were stern – they were good, but they were stern – and they told me to lie down, but I wasn't going to shut my eyes, no way! I remember I was concerned as well that I was getting blood all over this guy's garden furniture, I recall him telling me, 'Don't worry about that, son!' They got me on a stretcher, over the hedge, and into the helicopter. They gave me an injection of some description, I'm not quite sure what, but then I was on my way to hospital. One funny aspect of that incident, which I discovered long afterwards, was the fact that the nose of my fairing with the number one plate on it was stuck in the hedge where it had flown off in the impact. When the practice session was red-flagged, one of the other competitors who was stopped on the road spotted it there, picked it up, put it inside his own machine and took it home with him. I never got that back and as far as I know he's still got it. I keep meaning to have a word with him about it!

That was the worst I'd been bust up in any smash I'd ever had. I'd dislocated my shoulder, broken some bones and the cuts I had were deep. The broken bits were complicated as well. There was a lot of scar tissue and bone debris inside the shoulder. I'd fractured my joint and the shoulder blade, as well as dislocated my shoulder. On top of that, the dislocation had been out for over four hours, because when I was first flown in on the helicopter, the medics had initially tried to put it back in without me being under anaesthetic, and they couldn't manage to do it. I suppose all the muscles and tendons around it had tensed up by then. So it was out of its socket for a long time, and while it was out a lot of the damaged bits and bone fragments had settled into where the shoulder should have been. When the shoulder finally went back in, after they had put me under, it went back in on top of all this debris.

I decided briefly then while I was in hospital that I was going to give up racing, but the reasons for that were more financial than anything else. It's always a depressing time when you're in hospital after a crash, and you know your bike is wrecked, thinking, 'Every penny of my life practically is tied up in that machinery.' If it's destroyed, it's destroyed – that's it gone. Then you've got a doctor telling you that you may not ever be able to ride a motorbike again, maybe that's what they say to everybody, maybe that's what they hope! You know you're going to need operations. Hours take a long time to go by when you're lying in hospital, so I was probably feeling sorry for myself, thinking, 'Well, that's a life-changer.' I came to the conclusion that the first thing I would have to do when I got out would probably be to put the house on the market. I was self-employed and there was no way I was going to be able to work for a long time, probably several months – and, as it turned out, a lot more. Luckily I had an insurance policy which paid out almost enough to cover the mortgage, but not enough to live on. I've never claimed the dole, and never wanted to, so I ended up flogging off whatever I could sell out of my garage, things like tools, bits of equipment that I had which people wanted. It was stuff I really wanted to keep but at that point I had no choice.

I gave an interview for the newspapers during race week in which I told them that I thought Craig and myself were the luckiest two guys at the TT for having walked away from that crash. I said that I wasn't gutted or upset by the fact that I had waved goodbye to the British Championship title that I had been chasing that year, but I think I was putting a bit of a brave face on things for the benefit of the newspapers. The bike that I had crashed on was back in my garage by that point. I sometimes like to go in there and not do anything but sit there, and think, and having this wreck in the garage wasn't doing my head any good at all. In fact it was pretty depressing having that burned out thing sat there next to me. At one point I was having a conversation with my brother, and I told him that I was going to get a skip and dump the thing in it, because as far as I was concerned it was just scrap. I think that it was him who first suggested that I give the Manx Museum a ring to see if they would be interested in it.

Initially I was a bit sceptical, and doubted that they would really want a wreck of a sidecar. Nevertheless I made the call, and on this occasion my timing was spot on. I had no idea that at that moment they were in fact in the process of planning a major exhibition for the following year. The museum was looking for a centrepiece for that display, something dramatic which summed up both the glory and the danger of the TT. The machine that I was going to dump down the tip turned out to be it, and thousands of people who went to the museum saw that bike as a result. I don't know anyone who saw that exhibition who didn't comment on my bike being in it.

Meanwhile Noble's Hospital had told me that I would definitely need surgery, but they said it could be up to nine months before they could do anything with my shoulder, then they said there would be a good three-month recovery period after that, but that would be recovery up to the point where I could then start to train and get fit. That meant that racing in the TT Centenary in 2007 would definitely be out of the question. Noble's did a great job of putting me back together in the first place, but to me the urgency that was driving me along was the need to get myself back into racing as quickly as possible. I was going to the hyperbaric chamber in Douglas every day to help heal my wounds, and my cuts in particular. I didn't want to have a skin graft and I was having the dressings changed every day at Ramsey cottage hospital. The hyperbaric chamber compresses the oxygen in the air that you are breathing, so that you take in more and that encourages the healing process. While I was at the chamber one day a kind lady there asked me if I was having any physiotherapy for my injuries. I said, 'No, the hospital have told me that I've got to keep it fixed, with no movement.' She said, 'Well, if you don't move it, it will only get worse. I think you should ring Isla Scott in Peel.' So I phoned up Isla, who is a well-known physiotherapist on the Isle of Man, specializing in sports injuries. The first thing she said was, 'I wondered when you were going to ring me!' She fitted me in for an appointment, and after that I went there for an hour-long appointment every working day for six months. I never missed a day, but after four weeks of treatment she said I needed to be looking at an operation, and that I needed to get things moving in that direction quickly. With the best will in the world I wasn't going to be able to get the surgery done in the time frame that I needed on the NHS in the Isle of Man, and that meant getting the operation done privately through a specialist. I got myself an appointment with Dr Lennard Funk, a South African surgeon based in Manchester. I arranged a consultation with him, I flew over there and I got the last appointment of the day. He looked very tired, like he'd had a long day. I think he just wanted to go home really, but I arrived there and told him Isla had sent me – he knew her very well – and he said, 'Oh yes, you're the motorbike rider, let's have a look.' He had a look at my shoulder, but he wasn't at all happy. He explained to me that every dislocation should have a clean-out process before the joint is put back in, but of course that's not possible in every single case! Noble's had to get this dislocated arm back in, and there was more than one person getting flown into the hospital on the day that I was injured; they were a bit busy!

He also said that he didn't think he should go into my shoulder while there was so much nerve damage. He felt that the injury was too complicated, and offered to refer me to another surgeon in London. I said to him, 'Surely if you're saying that, then they're going to say that too.' I continued, 'I'm willing to take the chance if you're willing. I know I could lose a lot of time or money but it's me that's losing it, it isn't you!' It's important to remember that the only other operation I'd ever had in my life up to that point was when they put me under anaesthetic to put my shoulder back in when I first did the injury, so I was pretty worried about it, but at the same time I wanted it done! I said to Dr Funk, 'Look, here's how serious I am – if you said to me that you could get me on the operating table within the hour, then I'd say go ahead and do it. I'm scared, and I'm worried about the outcome, but I haven't got a choice, I need this done and you're my only option.' He said, 'Well, if you're willing to understand that it might not work at all, we'll go ahead.' I knew he wasn't familiar with the Isle of Man or the TT, so I left a DVD of the 2005 races with him. I wanted him to see how important it all was to me. So that was the Tuesday, and I was booked in for the following Saturday for my operation.

I flew back on the Saturday morning, and when I turned up for my pre-med he came into my room really jolly and rubbing his hands together. He smiled and said, 'Watched the DVD, we've definitely got to get you fixed for next year's TT, haven't we?' He was all excited and he went on, 'While we're on the subject, I need you to get me a picture for my wall.' His wall in the surgery was covered in pictures of tennis players, rugby players and football players, people he had treated for sports injuries, so it was nice to be able to introduce him to motorcycle racing. He became a big fan of the TT and since then I think he's fixed a lot of motorcycle guys; some really big names as well, some world-renowned guys. It cost me a few grand to get the operation, but he fixed me, and got me straightened out. If it hadn't been for him and Isla Scott, I never would have made it to the 2007 TT, it just wouldn't have been possible!

I started working again in January 2007. I struggled on, about half a day at a time, and some days I had to leave it and come back to it later in the day. A shoulder injury is one of the hardest to get over, because it's not the socket that holds it together, it's held together by tendons and muscle and if they have been damaged, your arm is going to shake. I found welding a struggle. Dr Funk had told me that I would still feel the effects of that injury two years down the line, and in fact I still struggle with welding today. It's not as neat as it used to be – it does the job OK – but it doesn't look as tidy as it should sometimes, and I often swear at myself under my welding mask as a result! But I had to get on and build myself a new bike ready for that year's TT. The bike I had in 2006 was probably the best I've ever built. It was the third TT I'd done on it, and we'd developed it from a good bike into a great bike. In that time we increased its lap speed by over 30 seconds in three years, and that's a massive chunk. If John McGuinness[18] could increase his lap speed by that amount, he'd be jumping for joy, that's the reality of it. But with the bike I built early in 2007, the chassis was great, it would go around corners just like my old bike, but it simply wasn't as quick. It didn't accelerate, it didn't get from A to B anything like as fast, and it was down on top speed considerably as well. That was purely down to our lack of time with that new type of Honda engine. We didn't get those new Honda engines until March of that year. So it left me a bloody small gap to get things built while I was still struggling physically. I was also trying to do the World Championships again at the same time, so I'd got far too much on my plate. I had Rick Long on the side; he was living in England at the time, so the technical side of things was falling heavily on me. Without the bike being ready, it couldn't be track-tested, therefore we couldn't move on with the engine development, and therefore it was not a particularly good package if the truth is known. In fact I'd go as far as to say it was one of the worst packages I'd ever put together. No one was at fault really, the only fault was that I'd injured myself. Maybe if I hadn't, and we'd just moved on to that newer generation engine, then we would have had more time to work on that new power plant, and it might have been a lot better, who knows? I'd certainly have been fitter, and I'd also have had more confidence, because that had also taken a kick up the ass as a result of my crash. The upshot of all this was that I missed the first practice of the TT that year, simply because the bike wasn't ready.

I was having trouble within the team as well. My brother as usual was there doing a great job, but other people were making it extremely difficult. There was an obvious lack of interest in some quarters, and I felt like I was on my own trying to achieve this bloody TT win, and on achieving it the rest of the season just fell apart for the same reasons. I've no time for anybody who won't try to equal the effort that I'm putting in. So having overcome all of that, I feel quite proud of the fact that we won those two races at the 2007 TT. We won those races purely because we finished them. I suppose that year changed my outlook a little bit on how you win a race. In the past I was always hell-bent on wanting to set the track alight, to be the fastest, but sometimes things have to be dealt with in a different way. If the bike ain't good enough then you're not going to be the quickest thing out there, but in spite of that we still achieved two wins at the Centenary of the TT. It will always be there in history, set in stone.

It's fair to say, though, we had a disastrous practice week in 2007, one of the worst. We missed the first practice session on the Saturday because we were still getting the bike ready. We went up to Jurby airfield on the Sunday to test it; we had a brand-new race engine in, and when we ran it one of the con rod bolts broke. The con rod went out of the front of the engine, and this brand-new engine was instantly destroyed. We only had two tuned engines and now one of them was wrecked. We wanted to have the other tuned engine checked over, to make sure that there was nothing loose or wrong there as well, so we had that one stripped down. Meanwhile one of our sponsors paid for a brand-new CBR600 road bike from Tommy Leonard's dealership, and we pulled the engine straight out of that and put it in the outfit, just so that we could go out on the Monday night for practice. We just did a slow lap of practice, we just toured round that night but the suspension was all wrong so that needed some more work. It turned out that our other tuned engine was fine so we put that back in, went out on the Tuesday night with it, and an ignition sensor broke on it. I think it was Wednesday night before we really seriously got going. On Thursday we put a quick lap in, but we'd had a dreadful week and were something like 10 horsepower down on our 2006 bike, which is massive, a huge amount. Clive Padgett, the motorcycle dealer and sponsor from Batley, was good enough to lend me a MoTeC engine management system, and a wiring loom. Well, the wiring loom is made to go on a solo, not a sidecar, so it was never going to be a case of simply slotting it in. Clive said I could borrow this item of kit, but only after practice week. They cancelled the first sidecar race on the Saturday, and that gave me time. I went straight round to him, got this thing and I spent all night on it. I didn't go to bed on Saturday night, I spent all night fitting this thing and altering the wiring loom and the clock set to go on it. The following morning we went out at Jurby airfield to set it up, and eventually we got it going, but it was still way off the pace.

We went off in the first race, and with our lack of power I knew that it was just a matter of time before Nick Crowe[19] came past us, which he did. But then he had an engine problem of some description, and went out, and at that point I thought, 'Right, get your head down.' With all that had gone on, I was bit deflated, though – I wasn't myself at all. That crash the previous year definitely had an effect on how I was thinking and feeling, but so did the practice week. It was far from being a good team effort. Anyhow, at that point in the race I saw we had a board saying we were third, and then I got another board saying we were second and that was at half distance. It was halfway round the second lap, and I thought, 'Fucking come on,' I remember properly shouting at myself inside my helmet, shouting, 'Pull your fucking finger out!' and off we went *whoosh*, and we won it from John Holden by something like 5 seconds. The two HM Plant Honda solo riders, John McGuinness and Ian Hutchinson, had one spare CBR 600cc engine to share between them. In the intervening spell between that first sidecar race and Race B it came to a point where they knew they didn't need it, so Neil Tuxworth, the Honda team manager, offered it to us. He said, 'If you want to try it, it's just sat there.' So we put it in, from memory we put the throttle bodies on it as well, but it's hard to say if it went any better than what we already had.

Race B came around and with it came another incident blown up by the press. We got into the warming-up area, and the rev counter – the clock set – started jumping around with the gauge going up and down. My friend Nick Oldfield, who helps me with wiring, was there and he said it was a loose connection. He ran off, got a soldering iron, stuck it in, and it was sorted, or so it seemed. We got out onto the grid, the 3-minute board went up, and the clock started going haywire again. I said to Graham, 'Run down and get the other clock.' So he legged it down to the paddock, came back with the spare, by that time I'd undone the first one and we put the other one on. But in the meantime they had announced a 5-minute delay in starting the race because they were trying to catch some dog that was running loose on the track! Well, the papers wrote afterwards that this dog had saved my race, and that if I was an animal lover I would have adopted it, and all this other bullshit. That bike would have operated 100 per cent fine with the first clock! The only thing I wouldn't have been able to see was how many revs it was doing and what temperature it was running at. It's not an essential part, and you don't look at it half the time anyway. I guarantee you that there wasn't a single rider there who would not have gone out just because that thing wasn't working properly, but I was just pissed off with it. I thought, 'Fuck it, change it!' and I'd already started unscrewing it – I think – when that 5-minute delay was shouted out. But some people got it into their heads that the delay was actually arranged deliberately to help me out, or whatever.

Anyway, we got away at the start of the race and it was a similar story to the first outing of that TT. Nick Crowe was streaking away with it for the first two laps, but sidecar racing is as much about tactics as anything else, and sometimes when you go for speed you sacrifice reliability, that's the trade-off. I just thought, 'I'll keep my head down and ride my race, and see what happens.' Back in early 2006 we had been leading the British Championships. Wet or dry track, we were miles ahead. We were more than just dominant then, we were streets ahead of the rest of the pack. Maybe as a result of that we were over-confident at that point, I don't know. I do know that we went into that 2006 TT full of confidence, we ended up having an accident, the outcome was carnage, and I don't think I've been the same kind of rider since then. I definitely have had a different approach to racing in the years that have followed. It's more of a clever approach, I feel, and this is where Rob Fisher was so good. Rob had a certain air of intimidation about him. While we were friends in one area of life, we were also full-on rivals in another. He would sometimes approach things (and he's never told me this, but I know it's true!) thinking, 'I ain't going to be as quick as Dave here, but I can rattle his cage! I can keep the pressure on, and just maybe it will come my way.' Sometimes that's what you've got to do. Well, that's what I chose to do in that second race. I just kept the pressure on Crowe, he knew I was behind him pushing him, and sure enough on the last lap at Ballahutchin he blew his engine. I came in to take my thirteenth win at the TT, and it was a historic moment, taking a double victory in the 100th anniversary of the event.

I rode in the Champions' parade on the Friday after the Senior race, but I didn't go round on one of my own winning machines, instead I used a replica of George O'Dell's. The money that O'Dell had raised when he came over to the Lido in 1977 had helped me get started in racing and so I thought of him in a funny sort of way as my first sponsor. As years went on I never really gave much heed to anniversaries, but as it loomed up I thought, 'Bloody hell, a hundred years of TT racing!', and of course not only that, it was thirty years exactly since O'Dell had won the TT. Even more than that, he'd won the TT in the same year that he won the World Championship, which was a very rare thing to do. His passenger Kenny Arthur is still alive, so the idea came to me of building a replica of his bike. Before I did that, though, I tried damned hard to find the original bike. I must have made fifty or sixty phone calls up and down the country, trying to find that thing. I got sent from one place to another, I got told that it was hanging up from a barn roof, and that it was red rusty, or that it had been chopped in half and a different engine put in it, but could I find it? I was pissed off because even if I had just got one component from it, like a wheel even, it would have added more authenticity. But it was a total impossibility. If you think about it, a bike that could win the TT and the World Championship in the same year must have had some bloody clout! What's a real shame is that a bike of such historic importance, and which had also meant a lot to me personally, was either cannibalized or ended up in some bloody skip. It's sad. It's also sad the way that George lost his life. He lived for the sport he chose to do, and I suppose like me at certain points in my life, his personal life suffered, and things happened that shouldn't have done, and ultimately he lost his life. I thought it was shite that this guy was remembered mainly for that, when he did so many other great things. For me it was a combination of thoughts and emotions and feelings that led me to build this replica of his bike as closely as I could to the original, and ride it round the track on the centenary. I only rode it once, on one lap, but that was enough.

It was a fairly easy machine to build, because those things back then were pretty basic. I would have said it was about a 90 per cent accurate representation of the original. Even the guy who built the actual chassis that George had won on, Terry Windle, he looked at it and said, 'Jesus Christ, it's as near as dammit the same bike, it's startling.' There were so many people who wanted to parade that year that they had to have two parades. I did the Champions' parade after the Senior on the Friday, and I let Terry ride it in the Monday parade. I had lots of guys coming up to me that year, saying, 'Dave, it's just like going back thirty years.' So many people who used to race that kind of bike came up to me that year and told me that it was just like going back thirty years, and that it was just like the bikes they used to have. It attracted a lot of attention. To have Kenny Arthur with me on the side when I did that parade lap just put the cap on it for me, because he has great memories. He's in his sixties now but he had a great life in racing and he and his wife Chris went everywhere with the bikes, all over Europe. When he came to see it he was overwhelmed, he was over the moon about it. He comes to the TT every year. Every year he comes back to watch the racing, he's still into it. We went pretty fast on that lap in places but mostly I had to take it fairly steady, as I thought, 'I don't want to freak Kenny out here!' He hasn't ridden at the TT for twenty-five years or so and he had an accident a few years back, which made actively passengering the bike as he would have wished a bit difficult for him. But we pinned it pretty fast down Sulby Straight and up the Mountain Mile, and what I really enjoyed was coming out of Governor's Dip, because I raced it out of there. We were wheel-spinning out of the dip and halfway along the straight, and went flat out across the start–finish line. Just about everybody commented how fantastic it sounded. It was a real piece of nostalgia. That parade lap was so important to me that I was prepared to miss the first practice sessions of the British round of the World Championships to be in it. I'd put a lot into it. I'd spent two years building the bike, along with my old friend and sponsor Eric Bregazzi, because he also helped me put that sidecar together; it meant a lot to him as well.

I flew out at six in the morning on the Saturday after Senior Race Day, and we just arrived at Brands Hatch in time to qualify for that World Championship round. For the remainder of the season I just did the World Championships, or Superside as it was called that year, and I did it in the colours of Peter Lloyd. Peter is still a great friend of mine. He first introduced himself to me in 1998. He and his family had owned the Lloyds chemists chain in the UK, and he had just sold up and retired to the Isle of Man. Peter and his family are really big motorsport enthusiasts, they have a great collection of classic cars, but motorbikes were a new thing to them, particularly Peter. He lived nearby and we used to have a pint together occasionally in the local pub and became good friends. It was a social thing between us rather than any business thing, but one day he said, 'Why don't you have another go at the World Championships?' He and his wife funded that effort entirely themselves. Honda weren't interested in doing anything outside of the TT, and yes, they had backed me for several years and had been very good to me, and I'd been loyal to them. But we had been there at the World Championships in 2000 with this Honda engine and it was no good in that role, it just didn't suit the application, and that's fair to say. So it would have been wrong to go in there again with something we knew would struggle. Our sponsors would have been pissed off with it blowing up all the time, and Honda would have been pissed off because their name would have been on the side of it while it was blowing up all the time. So we'd been there, done that. Honda weren't interested in trying it, anyway, even with their new Fireblade engine.

So the Suzuki engine was the obvious choice to use, that was the winning engine and it works well in a sidecar, and naturally that was what we went with. Peter and Tracy Lloyd were sponsoring me with this, and they said, 'Whatever is the best, Dave, that's what you should have.' And that was what we got. Peter even bought a second bike halfway through the season to try and help me, because I was still getting over my injuries and it was a far more physical bike to ride than my TT bike. I struggled to ride it, and I felt like I'd let him down massively. He had high hopes, it was a one-off thing this, it wasn't going to happen again. This particular time Peter was able to help me; for him it was the right year, while for me it was the wrong year. It was just the way it fell. Maybe I shouldn't have accepted the sponsorship, looking back on it, because I couldn't do it justice. I really could not do it justice, simply because I wasn't fit enough. The other problem was that I wasn't aggressive enough either. I'd lost that aggressive edge I used to have; it had gone in the 2006 crash probably. I was always worried about crashing Peter's bike or damaging it, or turning it over, whereas in reality Peter wasn't bothered about that. If we'd damaged it, we would just have fixed it! I felt like I wasn't doing the whole job justice. It was very difficult for me to accept that, but I was going to races where I should have finished in the top six easily but I was finishing twelfth! I was embarrassed at my own performance, to be truthful, but I just had to keep going, in the hope that it would get better. It did get better, towards the end of the year, but to cap it all I was having personal problems in my life which screwed up my racing for a while as well.

We went to some great race venues that season, though. We went to the Sachsenring, a purpose-built track, and the Nürburgring, both of which are in Germany, and the Salzburgring in Austria, a real classic fast old track. We did have some great rides at some other circuits as well. We went to Rijeka in Croatia near the Italian border. It was a beautiful place, with a great track. I was sixth there. This was at the end of the year, so things had just started to come together a bit. We went to Le Mans, a fantastic circuit, we had a great race there and I finished in sixth place there as well; that was my last World Championship race that year. We had a great engine in the bike, we had got it handling reasonably well, and I was at last getting a bit of fitness back, so I could run with the faster lads at least for a number of laps before I started dwindling off a bit. By the end of that year, 2007, we were bloody fast again. I'd got Dan Sayle back on the chair with me, and he found it a good new challenge to an extent. We won a few races at the end of the year, at National level, in England and at Pembrey in Wales, and so on. We were putting in lap times that were putting us on a par with some of the leading drivers in the world. We were right up there with Tim Reeves[20] and Ben Birchall's lap times – like at Pembrey, for example, we were right on it. But I couldn't carry it on. I went into the next year and things weren't going too well in any area for me. I was still having problems in my personal life, and I struggled on the racing side as well. There was a lack of funds that made that increasingly hard. All in all it was a very difficult time.

For the 2008 TT I chose to ride a Suzuki rather than a Honda-powered outfit. This was because after 2007 I was so disappointed with a lot of things that were going on, both in my personal life and in my racing, that I thought, 'I need a *radical* change here.' So I decided to drop the Honda thing and go with something that I knew would be bloody hard work but which would give me a new challenge, and that was to go with Suzuki. I thought, 'Move on, and get the Suzuki engine.' No one had ever won a sidecar TT on one, and I wanted to try and do it. The Suzuki power plant wasn't exactly an unknown quantity, however – there were numbers of other competitors using that engine at the TT and doing pretty well with it. But I don't tend to look at my nearest rivals, and wonder what they are doing, because they are the people I want to beat! I tend to look a lot further afield to see what the trends are. I look at the World Championship series, and the World Supersport Championships, and the most powerful bikes are the ones at the front! Back at the TT, the TAS Suzuki team were winning races using the Suzuki 600cc engine, which was the one I was thinking about using. Apart from my other motives for moving on to Suzuki power, I just didn't feel that the newer generation of Honda engine was the right thing for a sidecar. I know that there are guys using them today, and they are very fast, it's true, but I think it's fair to say that it takes a lot more work to make them fast! Overall, I just thought that I had come to the end of the road with Honda. It wasn't just the new engines; there were also changes in management at Honda UK which made it more difficult to get the kind of support that I was used to having. I had been used to working with some guys who were *really* into it. They were as much into the sidecars as they were the solos, and I'm talking about guys like Bob McMillan, Dave Hancock, and Mark Davies who took over from Bob McMillan. I could ring any one of those guys if I wanted to; I could ring up Dave Hancock, who was head of Research and Development, and speak to him directly and you can't get much better than that. I could phone Mark Davies, who was then general manager of Honda UK. I could phone him at home and talk to him like old friends about any given situation. But those people moved on, and from then on things were less personal. I'm not a computer man, I don't communicate by email, and I don't even want to try. I like to pick up my phone and talk to someone, and if I can't, then I won't bother trying. I know that perhaps sounds pretty pathetic and stupid to some, but that's me and that's the way I like to communicate. Those three had been the sort of people that I could deal with in that down-to-earth way I like, but I hate being made to feel that I'm a bloody nuisance to somebody. After they went I started to feel like I was becoming a bloody nuisance, and that I was begging, and I don't ever want to be in that situation.

With those feelings, I began to think, 'My time is done here.' It had been a good few years with Honda, and I'd done my best on the equipment that they had supplied. They sponsored me in order to get TT wins, and TT wins is what they got. I enjoyed the support that I had during those years. I wouldn't go as far as to say that I couldn't have got by without it, because I'm the kind of guy who would have got by without it. But I'm more than grateful for the support that I got from them, and more so the friendship which I got from the guys I've just mentioned, because when I crashed in 2006 two of my first visitors in hospital were Dave Hancock and Mark Davies. When I actually thought that I wasn't going to be able to get back into racing because of the cost of getting things back on track, it was those guys who basically pulled it together. It was their support that got it going again. But they were finding it more and more difficult to justify the kind of support we needed within their own organization. It wasn't like the situation with a solo team, who would just have been given a couple of road bikes and told to get on with it. Running a sidecar demands more than that, so it was becoming very difficult for them within Honda. In the end I just thought, 'That's it, we've got to move on here.' I phoned up Dave Hancock and told him, and he completely and totally understood, in a friendly way. It wasn't like a business dealing. I never had a contract with Honda, it was just an agreement between a bunch of guys who became friends; between a big corporate company and me, a little guy in his garage. Looking at it cynically, to them I was cheap. To gain that amount of TT wins with a solo team would have cost them Christ knows how much. But at the end of the day I was more than grateful for the help I'd received, because it kept me doing the thing I loved. From me there were no hard feelings, and certainly no animosity. Why would there be? I'd enjoyed a lot of support from them and they'd had some good results from me. They'd supplied and I'd delivered, and that was what it was all about. It wasn't really about anything else, but all things come to an end, so I moved on. The Suzuki thing was a new challenge, and I wanted to try it.

I got in touch with Suzuki GB, and told them I was planning to run the Suzuki engine in my TT outfit. I told them it was something I fancied doing and I wondered if they were interested in joining up with me and giving me a bit of support, which they did. They were interested straight away. I had a meeting with some of the top people there, and they supplied me with race kit parts, things like that, to put together this new bike. I think that Suzuki GB backed me, and gave me the gear, because they were desperate for some wins. They'd had a dry period, and apart from perhaps Bruce Anstey in the Superstock they hadn't got their name on the trophies much in the previous few years. It was a good bike that we put together using that engine, but we had teething troubles, as you always do with new machinery. I only got to race once before the 2008 TT, at Jurby road circuit, and the bike handled completely differently from what I was used to because of the way the engine was situated in the chassis. I then went into the TT with this new Suzuki outfit, but it was a difficult scenario because it was a completely new thing to me, completely alien to me really. I'd ridden it at just one meeting and then went straight on to the TT. To be honest, I'd put too much onto my plate again. I kind of expected too much of myself, and I'd thought to myself, 'We can win with this.' The reality was I'd never ridden with that engine before and the chassis was also totally different to what I was used to, because it had to be in order to accommodate that new engine.

We had a tough practice week in 2008, with constant electrical faults. It turned out that the MoTeC engine management system we used wasn't compatible with a lot of Suzuki's own electrical sensors. It was something we only found out during practice week, that over a long distance like the TT course these components got hot and started to break down. If you could pit stop for a new sensor every lap it would have been fine but we couldn't! It took us all week to try to sort these problems out and even by race week we still hadn't fully got to grips with them. We broke down in the first race because we'd had an engine fault right in the last practice session, on the night before the first race, and we'd been up till three in the morning trying to sort this fault out. The engine was then put back together out of two other engines to try and get around this fault, and in the process of reassembling it the clutch didn't go back together correctly. We had no time to test it, we had to go straight out onto the grid on the following morning, and the clutch slipped as soon as we set off from the line. But still we were second in Race B that year. We put that Suzuki outfit round at over 115 miles an hour in that race, and we finished second behind Nick Crowe. That bike then was as good as it was going to be at that time, but it was still far short of its real capability, and I knew that potentially it was capable of a lot more. I then did several short circuit meetings, but in the twelve months that followed I think I only did eleven races. Nevertheless, we developed the bike over that time, got rid of the MoTeC engine management system and went for one of Suzuki's own engine management systems. That worked a hell of a lot better, and as it turned out it made the bike a winner.

Directly after the 2008 TT, I went through one of the most difficult periods that I'd ever experienced in my personal life. Most of what has been written about it in the newspapers is frankly bollocks, but I feel that I have been judged very harshly by some people as a result of that. All that I really want to say about that chapter in my life is firstly, don't believe everything that you read in the newspapers, and secondly that there are two sides to every story. There is no doubt, though, that this incident affected my outlook and my racing. I took some time off and had a good long think about whether I even wanted to carry on with sidecars, and what I wanted to do with my life. Nevertheless, we went back to the TT in 2009, and won it on that bike with a Suzuki engine and set a new race record, which still stands today. That was a great experience, because starting out with a brand-new venture and producing a bike that could win the TT after only eleven outings was a pretty good achievement. Being realistic, that's an incredibly short space of time to get a new package up to that standard, but there are no shortcuts. On the run-up to the event a local businessman, Andy Faragher, had stepped in to support us with some finance, to help us get a more competitive package together. We got two new engines together, and had them race-tuned, but the advice that the tuner took from what was considered to be a reliable source turned out to be wrong. Through no fault of his own, the tuner had been given wrong information, and as a result these two engines that had been paid for by Andy Faragher turned out not to be up to much. In preparation for the event we'd also had some other engines that had failed. They were fast, but they'd failed. So in the weeks prior to the TT we'd had fast engines that had failed, and slow engines that had also failed. We thought, 'What the hell do we do?' Well, it was a joint decision by myself, Dan Sayle and my brother Graham to just do something between us, so we took these engines, stripped them down, and took what we thought were the best parts of each, put them all together and created this one engine which turned out to be not only reliable but fast as well. We went on to win Race A in the 2009 TT and to set the existing race record, over 115 miles an hour over three laps. None of us are engine builders or tuners, but there was a lot of common sense going on there. It made sense to us the way we put that engine together, and the guy I sold the bike to is still using that engine, it's still going strong, so something was very right there. It was a beautiful bike to ride.

In the 2009 TT only one of the two sidecar races was completed. In Race B I started as number 2 and Nick Crowe started as number 1. In the first race, after he had broken down on the second lap at Greeba Bridge, I went on to win quite easily. So after that the scene was set for Race B to be an absolute show-stopper. It had the makings of a classic head-to-head battle on the roads. It certainly started out that way, but unfortunately never reached a conclusion. We were almost equal, Nick Crowe and myself, up until the point that Nick crashed at Ballacob, on the way into Ballaugh. I remember coming around Alpine Corner, and just getting myself back to the centre of the road going past Ballakern Farm, when I saw a blanket of white smoke going down towards Ballacob. My first thought was, 'His engine has blown up again.' So I dabbed the brake and rolled the throttle just to ease off, and the next thing I saw was a piece of his fairing floating down out of a tree; I knew that it was bodywork, and that was the first indication I had that something was seriously wrong here. Now I stood on the brakes, went through the gears and brought the machine down. There was less than 10 seconds between us and Crowe on the road, so there was barely any reaction time. There would certainly have been no time for any of the marshals to react, because it was all just too quick. So there were no flags out, and we were literally on top of the scene of this accident within seconds of it happening. On entering into the smokescreen we saw that there were pieces of burning bike all over the road. Nick was lying in the middle of the road, and I passed within a couple of feet of him. I couldn't see his passenger Mark Cox anywhere, but the bike was scattered all over the road. It really did resemble what I imagine an aircraft crash to look like. There wasn't a clear path through the debris at all, and the bike was thump-thumping over pieces of wreckage as we went on. I toured through the scene of the accident, but as I did so Dan Sayle gave me a slap on the back, and gestured at me to crack on. It came into Dan's mind before it came into mine that there were bikes following us, and the smokescreen might well have cleared by the time they arrived on the scene; oblivious to what had happened, they could easily race on through, and plough into the wreckage and into us if we were only touring.

I think I'd got to Ballaugh Bridge before I picked up the pace again. I suppose with hindsight I should have stopped there to inspect my own bike for any damage it might have sustained from the debris in the road, but I had a lot going on in my head at that point. As you can imagine, when you've just seen something like that it takes a while to sink in. One thing I did have fixed in my mind, though, was there was no way that in the next twenty minutes that amount of carnage could be cleared up, not by any number of marshals, so I had a strong feeling that the race was going to be stopped; I didn't particularly feel like racing on anyway at that point. I picked up the pace a little bit and got into Ramsey, and it was at that point coming up out of Ramsey Hairpin that we saw the first yellow flag. As we were first on the roads I couldn't imagine that there was anything in front of us to slow us down, so I could only connect this to the crash. I suspected we were going to be pulled in. As we got up on to the mountain every single marshalling point had yellow flags out, so there was no doubt by now that the race was going to be stopped, and I knew that the Bungalow was the only place at which they could pull in a lot of bikes at once. We got up to the Verandah, and as I approached I could see a red flag being held out ahead of us, but at that point John Holden and Tim Reeves – who were in a personal battle – came racing past me, only to see the red flag ahead of them. They had quite a tussle going on, and they must have thought that the yellow flags were to indicate that I was having problems, and that was why I was touring. So we were all pulled over at the Bungalow, and when all the bikes were gathered up there we were allowed to proceed at a touring pace back to the Grandstand. There wasn't much else for it but to hope that the accident wasn't as serious as it looked, but it turned out that it bloody was. Those guys were lucky not to have been killed; as it was, they were both seriously injured. The race wasn't going to be re-run that day, so I went out to the back of the Grandstand with my girlfriend, my brother and Dan. We went and got some chips, I think, but at that point a couple of policemen came and asked if I could come into the office to see if I could help them make sense of what had happened. I hadn't seen the crash itself, but I'd seen the immediate aftermath of it, so I was able to tell them what I knew.

I was back at the TT in 2010, but this time the machine I had chosen to ride was Kawasaki-powered. The Kawasaki thing came about in a way that was a lot more laid-back than some of my other moves. I'd decided that I was going to use the Kawasaki engine anyway, whether or not with any sort of factory backing. I'm coming up to the end of my career, it's possible that I won't be back at the TT in 2011, and I'll finish on the make of bike I chose to ride. It's a good time to bow out now, really, because it's coming up to the centenary of the mountain circuit, and I've also got my personal life sorted out. It's going great now and I'm seeing a different side of life. When I chose the Kawasaki it was with a few different things in mind. One, I've never won on one before; two, my father and George Oates raced on Kawasakis in the 1970s, it was their last racing machine; and three, Kawasaki have never won in the sidecar class at the TT. That was my aim, to win on this thing and make it successful.

I got in touch with Kawasaki UK, and told them, 'Look, I've bought myself this engine, I'm building this new bike around it, I felt like I'd got nothing to lose by giving you a call to see if you wanted to help, and to be involved in this thing,' and they were dead keen straight away. Their presence at the TT has fluctuated over the years, but then they are the smallest of all the Japanese manufacturers, they're not big. A lot of these companies try to spread themselves too thin. They are in all these championships all over the world and all of a sudden when things aren't going so well, they've only themselves to blame, because they are guilty of trying to stretch too far. There's a global recession right now, and I'd say focusing on one class would be a good move at the moment, in the current economic climate.

Kawasaki are good at that. They seem to say 'Enough's enough', and they focus on one particular class. When times are good they spread themselves a little further, but then they are the first to pull back when they aren't. To me that makes good common sense. I think, luckily for me, they are coming into a period when their product is doing very well. And it is luck, because they did have lean years in the recent past, because their product hasn't maybe been quite as good as some of their competitors. But right now in Supersport 600 and in Superbike they've got some seriously good equipment, and riders want to ride that bike. So I think they are in a great position at the moment to do very well in the domestic scene, in the world scene and at the TT. I think that it's obvious when you see Ryan Farquhar and Conor Cummins going as well as they do in the solo classes at the TT. We proved a point as well with this Kawasaki engine at the 2010 TT, we got the fastest lap of practice, fastest lap of the event, and barring my own mistakes we really could have won that TT. That's why I would like, if I could, to go back and put that right, because we can do it. There would be no better time than during the centenary of the mountain circuit in 2011. Already, after the one TT that I've done on it, a couple of top teams have all of a sudden started using Kawasakis, just because of what we did in this TT. But on the run into the 2010 event it came back to me that there was some typical paddock bullshit going on. The rumour was that there was a tote or a betting book going on how long we'd last before we blew this thing up. It even came back to me that some bloody idiot was telling people that it wasn't even a Kawasaki, it was a Honda under all that Kawasaki livery! What a load of bullshit! Some people are pretty small-minded sometimes, and that was one of those moments.

It's true that the bike I crashed in 2006 was probably the best and fastest I've ever ridden, and if I wanted to I could replicate that bike right now and go racing on it, but that isn't my objective. I need to keep going forward with what I'm doing; I've got goals that I've set myself, and if I did just replicate an old bike I'd be going sideways or even perhaps going backwards. My current bike, the Kawasaki, is fantastic. I'd say it handles just as well as my old bike. On paper, I'd say it's got more power, but there are still things about it that I need to gel together. In 2010 I think I would rather have not done the TT at all, than have done it without trying that new Kawasaki engine. All of a sudden I've got a new ambition. No one in the history of the TT has ever won the sidecar event on all four Japanese makes of motorcycle. We've won on Yamaha, Honda and Suzuki, and now I want to add Kawasaki to that list. Added to that, no one has ever won a sidecar TT on a Kawasaki, just as no one had won on a Suzuki before last year. We were the first ones to do that. Now I feel that Patrick Farrance, who's an ex-World Champion passenger, is probably better in his application than I am in mine. I had somebody there riding next to me who is excellent, one of the best in the world, and we've both got the same ambition. He's never won a TT, and I've never won one on a Kawasaki, and I want to. We went into it having done only three short circuit meetings in 2010, and we set the quickest lap of practice. All but for a bad choice of tuning on the engine, which was my choice, I feel that we really should have won that first race. But it was my decision to do what we did to the engine, and it was wrong, it was very wrong! It was wrong to the point where I actually wondered what the hell I'd done. But you can't just stop and put it right, you've got to ride through it. I was very slow on the first lap, and I found out later that some people were thinking, 'Is he that confident that he can just ride along, and then give it hell on the last lap?' Some people honestly thought I was foxing, and I find it amazing that people actually believed that's what I was thinking. Nothing could have been further from my mind! You've got to go at it like hell right from the word go these days! It's fair to say that it was slow first lap, slow second lap and slow on the third lap, but we still put it round at over 115 miles an hour on the last lap and came within a couple of seconds of winning. We were the fastest loser!

To be honest, in a strange kind of way I'm almost glad Klaus Klaffenböck won in 2010. I'm glad because I don't want to be part of something that's getting so predictable that people are bored shitless watching Dave Molyneux win, or before me Nick Crowe, or before that Rob Fisher. Things do have to change, and I think it's healthy for the sport for there to be different winners. Personally, on a selfish level, I think it's healthy for me to be beaten occasionally as well. In the late 1990s and early 2000s I went through a stage where I had the TT so tightly by the scruff of the neck that there were almost two levels, me and the rest, and to be absolutely truthful I was getting bored with it. I was actually bored with racing, but I carried on doing it because that's what I did. I wouldn't say I didn't *want* to do it, but I was doing it because it was there, because it was on my doorstep, and because I could do it. It's funny, really, because my whole outlook has changed now; in a way I've got almost back to where I started. I've got to ride bloody hard now to win a TT race. If I couldn't win those two races at the 2010 TT, then I'm glad Klaffenböck won them, I really am. One, for the reason that I've just given; but for another reason, because he's a foreigner and not a British rider, and that has got to be one of the best things that could have happened for the Isle of Man TT. Not only is it good that a continental rider wants to come here, but more than that, he's an ex-World Champion. For someone of his stature and his background to come here and win the TT is *massive*. I think the importance of it might still be underestimated. I look at him and think, 'Well done, boy', because he has tried and tried and tried to succeed here. I think some people believe he didn't try hard enough at times but I can guarantee them that he did. He definitely tried hard enough, but at times it just didn't work for him. His only finishes have been brilliant ones, and his performances this year have been fantastic. It was a superb result. He bettered John Holden, Simon Neary, and Tim Reeves; these are fantastic drivers and teams. He bettered those guys, and that was outstanding. That's why I wasn't disappointed this year – I made a mistake, I should have stuck with my practice set-up and I didn't. I paid the price and I finished second. I think Patrick was disappointed because he firmly believed in my ability to overcome a deficit like that, but this is the way the TT is now. It's hard. It's competitive and it's hard. The standard in the sidecar class is extremely high. I might not be as fast as I used to be, in fact I know that I'm not, but I'm still eager to win, and I have to work hard for that now.

I felt like I was being interrogated by Tim Glover after Race A of the 2010 TT. If I don't win, it's almost as if the number one question is 'Why?!' There's almost an air of 'Why didn't you win, what went wrong?' Well, you can't win them all. We nearly won that race but we didn't. We were beaten by a World Champion, and we had a World Champion behind us in third. I like to say that I finished that race in a World Champion sandwich, and that's great, that has to be good for me, as well as for the TT. It's a huge hassle to come all the way to the Isle of Man so it has to be good for the event that two former World Champions want to make the effort to come here and compete. You have to think about it: Klaus Klaffenböck is a very successful businessman. He doesn't need to go racing to make a living, that's for sure. He's doing it because his heart is in it. It's in his family, a bit like the way it's in mine. One thing I do know about him is that he is an extremely determined man who will go to great lengths to achieve what he wants to achieve. He hit a stroke of luck when he got Dan Sayle on the side, because Dan is an absolutely outstanding passenger, one of the best of his generation. So they've got a great team together and I like that; I don't want an easy win, I want the hardest win I can possibly get, and if it means coming second or third sometimes then that's fine with me. At the end of the day they've got a great team together, have those guys, and it's for me now to up my game, and I'm up for that. More than. It's given me a breath of fresh air, it's taken away the monotony and the boredom, which was there, but isn't there now. I think back to riding against Nick Crowe. He was a fantastically talented rider, he had some great machinery under him and was a very difficult man to beat. He beat me fair and square in 2008. Tim Reeves is in that position now, he's got so much determination to win, Simon Neary likewise. John Holden at fifty-three years old is still desperate to win a TT, it's his ambition. So there is a lot of great competition.

Having said all that, I don't think the sidecar class at the TT is in a great position at present, because it's far too expensive. The money isn't around to back it. For whatever reason, big corporate companies don't want to back sidecars. This has been a really boring, pain in the ass situation for too long now. Of course, people like me, or Steve Webster, or whoever will be totally biased towards our chosen sport and think, 'Why the hell can't a corporate company see the potential of what a sidecar has to offer?' But it's true! Why can't they open their eyes and see what the sport has got to offer? In fact, I really do wonder how we've come as far as we have without decent backing. The end result of this is that there aren't enough young guys starting in it, and there aren't enough guys staying in it, because there isn't enough money around it for them to keep going. The TT and the people who run it have to be given a lot of credit for being the last of the old-school events in the world, because they are prepared to help the riders to try to compete. They offer reasonable start money and they put up a decent prize fund, it's respectable and it reflects what you're doing. I think so anyway, I'm happy with it, though others may not be. It would be good if we could make it easier, but I'm afraid it's getting harder. Even I can't attract a big financial sponsor at the moment. Kawasaki provide me with an engine free of charge, which is great, it's nice to have a manufacturer involved in the event who is interested to that extent, but they haven't really got the finances to put into it.

Sidecar racing is in a difficult place at the moment. People can't afford to go racing, and it's as simple as that. The real danger is that if we can't get a decent-sized TT grid together, then the organizers are going to struggle to run a race. I honestly don't know where that's going to end up. All I do know is that when I started in 1985 I was at the back of the grid as number 93, and there were fewer than half that number of bikes on the grid in 2010. That's scary, for the future. Regarding the ability that's out there now, it's probably better than it's ever been. In terms of competition, it's probably more competitive than it has ever been, and the machinery is better than it has ever been. Some people say that's part of the problem, that the machinery has become so high-tech that it has pushed out the people you might have got in the old days, who knew a bit about engines and could fettle them. I don't know. Rules and regulations for a class are always a bit of a controversial aspect. People tend to think you've got a vested interest if you keep shouting your mouth off about it, but my only vested interest is that a sidecar keeps racing around the Isle of Man TT circuit. If we don't sort the rules and regulations out for this class once and for all, and make it affordable, then I'm afraid it's in trouble. I know 'affordable' is a difficult word because there will always be someone who can afford it and someone else who can't, but there are simple measures which could be put in place to make it just more practical and sensible. People might then want to start racing again.

I get asked my opinion all the time, and to be honest I'm sick of giving it, because if it doesn't get laughed at, I get accused of having a vested interest. Now, I'll go along with whatever rules are laid out and I'll just ride my bike. I wish it was different, and that some of my ideas were taken seriously, because I think they are sensible. I've been accused in the past of dragging too much high-tech equipment into the sidecar TT, and of taking the rule book to the edge, and that's true, I have. I firmly believe that is what a bloody rule book is for at the end of the day, but I've always been *within* the rule book, not outside of it. I also firmly believe that I did take sidecar racing to another level. I've been told that by other people. I never thought that much about it myself at the time, but on thinking about it since, I definitely did change the outlook of sidecar racing in a lot of ways. But I'm not responsible for how much it has ended up costing. The people who make the rules are responsible for that, sometimes because they misinterpret the rules! There are things now that could be done, and it could be fixed, and it wouldn't cost people too much to adjust to those rules if they were changed slightly.

I'd like to be back in 2011 to win the TT, and to make history in doing it as well. If I retire from the TT after 2010, I think that it will be the enormous costs of racing nowadays that will have forced me to take that decision. It won't be lack of interest on my part, that's for sure. I love racing, it's in my heart, and maybe if I can't carry on at the top level with the TT I'll go into something like classic bike racing in the future. I look back on my racing career overall, and I think it has probably cost me more than I've gained from it. I've had a lot of abuse heaped on me over the years – unjustly so, I feel. A lot of that abuse has come via the internet, and I think that's one of the worst forms of communication ever invented. There is so much sheer gossip out there, it's impossible to respond to it or correct it, and I think that it's frankly out of order. I think if you want to say something, something important, then you should say it to someone's face. I'm pissed off that I seem to be the focus of attention in so many areas – in these internet chat rooms and forums – and ninety-nine times out of a hundred I'm misquoted. I'd like to know where half of these things that people think I'm supposed to have said have come from! I'm not a public person, I don't get up on my soapbox and shout my views, but at the same time, if someone really wants to know what I think, then I'm at the end of a phone. People can call me up, or most people know where I live, so they can call in and see me. People read things that other people have said about me on the World Wide Web and take it as fact, and it isn't at all! I perhaps wouldn't mind all of the personal abuse that has been heaped on me over the years if I had thousands of pounds stashed away in the bank as a result of the racing, but the fact is that I haven't. I've had to flog more or less everything I've won over the years just to keep going. Perhaps the only untarnished, positive thing which has come out of my racing career is the fact that one of my machines, the one which did the double at the 2007 Centenary

TT, is on display in the Manx Museum in Douglas. That means a huge amount to me, particularly as I know it will be there for all time, long after I'm dead and gone. Someone once described it as like one of the oil paintings in there. The artists are long dead, but the painting continues to live on, as evidence of the skills and talents that the artist possessed. I find that very flattering.

Looking back over my racing career, a lot of my greatest moments have been marred by some of the shit that goes on in the background, particularly at the TT. The first win I had in 1989 was really overwhelming. At twenty-five years old I wasn't really prepared for the emotional side of it. I hadn't done a lot of racing at that point, I couldn't afford to really, so it wasn't like I was in the thick of the National scene. When I did go over to England to race, I was overawed by the people around me, I felt I was beneath them, so that was a bit overwhelming, and the TT was much the same. The enormity of the thing takes a lot of getting used to, and you put so much effort into it. You start preparing for the TT two weeks after it finishes, you really are preparing for fifty weeks of the year. So when it does all suddenly go right, it's a lot to handle. That year, 1989, was a tough year emotionally anyway, with a lot of things that were going on. Winning that year was a massive thing; being told we had won and people jumping around for joy was great; but remember, we were initially told that we'd finished second, and I thought, 'Great, would have liked to have won, but great.' Then we were told we were first, so that's a very different thing from clearly being the winner from the moment you cross the finish line. The guy who thought he'd won it, he was pissed off. When that happens, the cream is off the cake. It's like the cake has fallen on the floor, then been picked up and given to you to eat second-hand!

In 1996, when we achieved so much at the TT, that was tainted as well. I'm extremely affected by what people say or do around me, and when I was being branded a cheat from as early as Monday night practice, that was extremely unpleasant. We spent all week in the guilty corner, and even though we proved everyone wrong, and won, it didn't make up for that. Even though it was satisfying, we never got to enjoy the real true emotion of winning it. It felt very strange, to be truthful, because I was fucking hacked off beyond belief, I can tell you. The sheer jealousy was one thing, but the cheat slurs were another. There has hardly been a year gone by when I've won a TT that hasn't been marred by some sort of crap going on in the background. But I'm as guilty as anyone, because I know that I should have grown out of this shit by now, and not been bothered by what people do or say. In 2005, when we set the first sub-20-minute lap, that was a massive achievement. That to me ranks among the biggest achievements in the history of the TT. That was a huge milestone, like 1996 was with the 110 mile an hour lap. What happened in 2005 was something that I realized was do-able in 1999, so it was a hell of a long time to wait. We came within one and a half seconds of doing that in 1999 on a bike that was in no way up to the job, so Craig Hallam and I must have been riding out of our skins that year. I was probably at the best I could be at that point, I was at the peak of my ability, taking into account my age and experience, and Craig was at the top of his game, he was a fabulous passenger. So to put us two together seemed to bring that sub-20-minute lap within reach. It shocked us how close we came, because we had no idea at the time. So I spent the next five years busting my ass trying to achieve that, and it just wasn't happening for one reason or another – weather, passenger, cancellation or whatever.

When it did happen, I didn't enjoy it. I enjoyed my ride at the 2005 TT, but I didn't enjoy what was going on around it, and in the background. I just don't get this idea of being backward at coming forward. We achieved *seriously* great things that day, and I don't mind saying it. People can say, 'He's full of shit, blowing his own trumpet again!' Well, yes, I'm going to, because I designed and built that bike, put together a great package, with a fantastic passenger, and did the first sub-20-minute lap. We won the TT and did the first three-lapper in under an hour. But simply because we'd set the track alight and simply because we had made history that day, when we went to the prize presentation that night we were booed. We were actually booed off the stage. I thought at that point, 'For fuck's sake, pick the pace up boys!' It was a strange emotion. All the ones that should have been right up there, were marred by something, it seems. In 2007 I had a pretty good year. It was a hard week, it was an uphill struggle, it was probably one of the hardest, but we were there at the end and we won it. I was a bit disappointed that I wasn't really fit to do the job properly. I was disappointed as well that the bike wasn't quite as good as my previous one, it wasn't as competitive and that was partly me and partly the engine, I suppose. I felt sorry for Nick Crowe and Dan Sayle that year, but they're not the first to be in that position where they've been leading both races, and then broken down. I've been in that position in the past.

When I won with Karl Ellison in 1993, that felt really good. I suppose it's fair to say I felt my biggest sense of achievement then. That was my first serious attempt at building a chassis, and we were good as a team; it was enjoyable. There was my brother Graham, Billy Quayle, Eric Bregazzi, and I had a good passenger in Karl. It was a bloody good team, and we enjoyed some good times with some good people. There were guys chipping in, people like Billy Boyd and the patrons of the Ginger Hall, and that felt good. We built this bike, went out, won both races and got the lap record on it, so that was great. I really enjoyed that, but it's hard to say apart from that which was the biggest or best win. I suppose back in 1993 I was a bit of an underdog, I was still largely unknown. By the time I got to the 2000s I think maybe people thought I was getting all these thousands in sponsorship and that they felt they could take pot shots at me as a result.

If I do decide to retire I'm sure I will carry on building bikes. However, I'd prefer to move into the classic scene, and away from the modern stuff. If I'm still involved in that scene, then the temptation to ride in it again is always there. I've got to a great place in my life now, I'm happier than I've ever been, and if I'm absolutely honest I am worried a little bit that carrying on with racing could damage that. If I do get into classic bike-building, I might even have a ride now and again, or take part in a parade lap. There are all sorts of classic events going on all over the world, where people can be successful or not so successful, it doesn't really matter. If they've got a bike to show off, that they want to go and ride, they can go anywhere, throughout Europe. The replica of the O'Dell machine that I built showed that there is a great enthusiasm for sidecar racing from a golden era, when times were good. Not so many people are building those kinds of machines, so maybe that's something I could get involved in, maybe there is a gap in the market there. Overall I'm happier now in my personal life than I've been for many years. I had a bad time for a number of years, and it took a long time to resolve itself. It was a really shitty situation. I don't give in easily to any difficulty, I'll go on and on in order to try to rectify a bad situation. But when you feel that something is going from bad to worse you have no choice but to get out. As luck would have it, I walked out of a bad situation straight into a good situation. I met someone, Justine, who I love very deeply. I wish I'd met her twenty years ago. We're married now, and we're putting together a nice home as a family. My intention now is hopefully to live a long life with her, we want the same things, we're moving in the same direction and for the first time in a long while I'm enjoying life!

Chapter 5

Constructor

Being a sidecar manufacturer has always been an ambition of mine. When I was eight or nine years old, my Action Men weren't soldiers, they were sidecar racers, slipped into PVC leathers which had been made by my mum, and put on home-made sidecars that I'd run like buggery down the road with on the end of a piece of string! I'd cannibalize any toys that I had which had suitable wheels, tear the hardback covers off books, lockwire a bit of eighth-inch welding rod onto the piece of book, and then fix the wheels on the axle. Toys back then had little chrome caps to fix the wheels on. So I'd build them at home, and I drew them every day at school, in the back of every book I possessed. To build a sidecar was my ambition, to build it and not just ride it but to *win* on it, and in particular to win the TT on it. To do that on something you have built yourself, that's what Honda do with a 10 million pound factory and 10,000 employees around the world backing them up. They are the kind of people who come to the Isle of Man and try and win, not people in a bloody shed, who work for themselves and who will spray a car to make ends meet. That's the reality of sidecar racing, and the fact that in this class you too can be a TT-winning manufacturer. You don't have to be Honda, Yamaha, Kawasaki or Suzuki to do it! I think as a manufacturer I've won twenty-one TT races. If three out of the top ten bikes which come in are mine, then I get a replica as manufacturer. It's nice when that happens, but I don't give it that much thought.

One thing that often surprises people about me is the fact that I don't work from blueprints or drawings when I'm building a sidecar. It's all in my head, but then it's all pretty basic stuff. I'm not working down to thousandths of an inch like a precision engineer. On certain little parts it's that precise, but mostly it isn't. The wheelbase is set at 60 inches. I've pulled the wheelbase back to 60 inches over the years from 64, which I started out at. That wheelbase length is a bit of a compromise between a short circuit bike and one that is designed for the TT. A longer-wheelbase bike suits the TT more, it rides the bumps better. A shorter wheelbase is more twitchy, but it's faster moving. It changes direction quicker because it is shorter. The longer it is, the slower it reacts. Not everyone likes my bikes, because they are so twitchy and light, but it suits my style of riding, and that of the people who buy them from me, I guess. The swinging arm pivot is set at 7¼ inches. Like the wheelbase length, I hit on a winning formula with that a number of years ago, by trial and error. I thought, 'I'm not going to get that any better, so I'll just leave it alone.' I'm not a trained engineer, and I guess an engineer would sit down and spend hours making a technical drawing, just to assemble exactly what I make out of my head. In my view it's so simple that it doesn't warrant blueprints. It's just a frame with bits hanging off it, and that's it. I start with my flat bench, which is all plumb and true and square, and I have three main jigs, which are metal frameworks that hold the headstock in position, the swinging arm pivot in position, and the sidecar wheel in position. I start with the main beam across the middle, that's the first section to go together, and I build it out from that. I've learned over the years that a lot of frame manufacturers will use an all-in-one jig, and build their bike completely within it, then when they have finished take all of the mounting points out, but that means the frame is too taut. It tweaks out of position when they remove it, because it's like an elastic band going off! I don't see the point of having a jig and doing it that way. A jig is to make sure everything is as perfect as it can be.

I build my outfits in three stages. The cross-section, the swing-arm pivot, is the first section to be finished. That is a finished piece. Then I mount the sidecar wheel, as the next piece, and the front is the last piece. The steel I use is hydraulic tube, which, exactly as its name suggests, is intended to contain high-pressure hydraulic fluid. You'd find it in the engineering trade – the Isle of Man Steam Packet Company use it, for example. It has fluid pumped through it, so it needs to be able to withstand high pressures. It's easily obtainable, readily available stuff. It sounds pretty crude but it's very flexible and workable. It will take a lot of vibration, and it will flex easily. My bikes have a lot of suspension built into them, but the cushioning is not just in the tyres and shocks, the whole frame has flex built into it. If you use stiffer material like an aircraft spec steel, it won't have anything like that flex and it will break. I once tried using a material called T45 but it snapped around the welds because it was too brittle. Some manufacturers still use it today, they still haven't learned. It's far better for a frame to have a lot of movement in it, because then it's less likely to break. It's important to remember that you aren't allowed any suspension on the sidecar wheel, and if you then have the bike suspension very soft, because you have to have it that way for a very stiff frame, it doesn't handle very well. So instead you run a very stiff suspension, but the frame and the tyres have their own suspension built in, so altogether you are getting a taut but flexible frame. It's almost a contradiction to say that, but it works!

In the past five years or so, manufacturers have also made engines a lot shorter and narrower and lighter. I've had to move the engine forward quite a bit to get it to work in the bike, but that has presented a problem, in that it makes the back of the bike very light. Engine structure can also vary radically from manufacturer to manufacturer – Honda, Kawasaki or whatever – so you have to bear in mind at the start what you are intending to use, because the chassis that I build will have to accommodate that engine. Some sidecar builders just make a standard bike which will accept any engine. The engine is just hung off engine plates, whereas with mine, the engine is an integral part of the structure of the frame of the bike, so that gives it a lot more strength. So, as I say, you need to take account of the type of engine you are going to use right at the very start of the build. Engines now are very different from how they were ten or twenty years ago. They are configured very differently now. They are built for a solo and designed to get the best out of a solo bike's handling, so when I adapt one for a sidecar I have to change quite a lot. When you adapt the engines for use in an outfit, you first need to cut the sump off, to try and get the engines as low as possible, given that you also have to have a certain amount of oil in there to keep it reliable. This gives the machine a very low centre of gravity and helps it to hold the road. Luckily, with the Kawasaki engine I'm using at the moment, I've been able to get it almost as low as it could possibly go. I also fit a series of baffles inside the crank case of the engine, and inside the sump as well. On a solo machine, when you corner the oil moves with the engine, and stays central within it. A sidecar is more like a car in that respect. When you corner, the engine stays level rather than tilting, so the movement forces most of the oil to one side of the engine or the other. This causes a lot of internal wear and tear on a sidecar engine, and the baffles help to reduce that movement of oil a little.

Some people use a dry sump system like they use quite often in car racing. A dry sump is in some cases an external oil pump, with an external oil tank, whereas a wet sump is one where the oil is gathered in the bottom of the engine and is sucked up by an internal pump. A lot of people think that a dry sump is the way to go with a sidecar. Maybe I'm a bit old-fashioned but I've got a great set-up here, one which doesn't give me problems. I get all the oil I need in there, and I've got the engine as low as I can possibly get it. Even if it had a dry sump on it, you still couldn't get the engine any lower. There are a few other modifications that you need to make to the standard road-bike engine to adapt it for sidecar use. You can't run the standard road-bike airbox unless you've got arms like a gorilla, because when you are riding a sidecar you've got to lie over the engine to reach the handlebars. The airbox is a pressurized system. The air enters through a vent in the bodywork on the outfit, passes through a filter system, then up into the airbox. The force with which it enters then pressurizes the air in the airbox, and then when the engine is on full tap it's drawing on that clean pressurized air for its oxygen, which increases its power. It forces oxygen into the engine, basically. Some systems work better than others, but we seem to have got it right, we've got plenty of air going into the engine, so there is plenty of power there. What I do with the airbox is something of a compromise: you have a very low bell mouth on the throttle bodies inside the airbox, because the airbox needs to be very low, so that the rider is very neat and aerodynamic, but also so that he can reach the handlebars. I've got short arms, so if I had this huge airbox sitting up in front of me I wouldn't be able to reach around and steer the bike. I may lose some power doing this, but what I lose in power I gain in rider comfort and being able to ride the bike properly.

All manufacturers are producing fuel-injected engines now. We've got more power out of the engines nowadays, but I think it's as much to do with the mechanical side of things as it is to do with the electronic side of it, meaning the fuel-injection system. Things have come on a lot, though, in the past ten years or so. I can remember over ten years ago Honda saying that they didn't think they could produce a better engine than the one they had produced that year, 1999. But ten or more years on, things have improved even further. The engines have to be road-bike based, four-cylinder 600cc four-stroke engines. You can do almost anything to them within your means, which I actually think is bad for the class. Sidecars are suffering at the moment through depleted fields and I believe it's down to the recession – there isn't enough money around and people can't afford to go racing every weekend. Most of them are doing it out of their own pocket, so the engines are something that needs looking at, but currently you can do pretty much anything to that engine provided it's a four-cylinder four-stroke engine.

I certainly don't think the problem is that the class has become too fast, not at all. In the 1980s at the TT the Formula One sidecar class was accused of being too fast, and in six years we were lapping miles faster than those machines on what was supposed to be a lesser machine. Now it's in a different world altogether in terms of speed, but it's just about at its limit. Without the rule book going in a different direction you can't make these things go round any quicker. In terms of speed, the thing has reached a natural limit, I believe, and some of the suggestions for making it slower wouldn't be practical anyway. It's no good putting a controlled treaded tyre on, because that would make it dangerous. The 600cc four-stroke engine is about the smallest you could use in the class; you really have to use engines which are available on the market. The next step down from that 600cc four-stroke would be a V twin engine, an SV650, or a twin-cylinder four-stroke 450cc. Yes, you could in theory run a sidecar class with those in, but I think that would kill it overnight. I think people would lose interest straight away. They wouldn't take up the challenge of building something new, and the cost would be more than what they've already got tied up in it. So, really, I don't think it would work. There is talk of running standard engines (engines straight out of a road bike) in the sidecar class instead of tuned engines. We tune our engines to the best of our ability – to the best of our financial ability as well – it's not quite as good as it could be but it's almost as good as it's ever going to be, given that we have to work within a budget. Also we have to think about the fact that it has to last three laps of the TT circuit, and some practice as well. If they made it so that we had to use standard engines, straight out of a road bike, that would be really good, but it wouldn't be much slower. It really wouldn't, because I've tried it and I've gone to within 2 miles an hour of the lap record, just using a standard engine.

If they do go to the standard engine rule, we won't then have to spend four or five thousand pounds on that engine in order to get the performance out of it. There is an argument that says that if we can't put an aftermarket part in it, then that engine might fail. It's a fair argument; yes, it might fail, but then again it might not! It's something we are going to have to try. But I know I'd rather go out at the start of the season with everybody on standard engines, and also able to afford to put new tyres and new brake pads in their bike. Basically it would mean people could afford to go racing again. Instead of having to spend four grand on their engine this month because they blew their last one up, those people would have the money to go to another three race events. As it stands at the moment, they spend that money on their engine, then can't afford to race it! There's a lot of common sense to be had out of all this. For the sport to survive and keep its head above water, and be taken seriously, I think the expense needs to be capped a little bit. It's a bastard because I'm obsessed with speed and performance, the faster the better, but it's at too big a cost, and that needs to be dealt with. For us to survive as a good strong class at the Isle of Man TT, which it has to be said is the backbone of sidecar racing in Britain, the rules have got to be adapted so that people can afford to race, not just at the TT but all year round so that they can gain their licence. It has also got to be affordable, so that people can think about starting racing in the first place. It's a formula, and the formula needs adjusting and being made suitable and affordable for everyone. By all means choose the engine you want. I'm not talking about having a one-make series, I don't like that idea at all, and don't support it. I believe that the people who are in Formula Two sidecar racing are people like me, who work five or six days a week, and those guys need to be able to afford to do it. On the safety side of it, when we are saving money on engine costs, it will make it safer, because there are too many guys, and I'm guilty of it as well, who've gone out there with a shit back tyre on because they can't afford to put a new one on. That's crazy because it isn't safe. It would help all round if the engine rules were standardized to take the cost out of it, and it's the running costs of the engine which are the main part of the problem.

Some people also argue that the aftermarket ignitions cost too much. Well, it's a matter of opinion whether you actually even need one of those. It's debatable, because I feel that manufacturers' electronics and engine control units (ECUs) are adequate for what we do in sidecar racing. I've proved that with my Suzuki win and with my Kawasaki in 2010. I won the TT in 2009 with the manufacturer's ECU on, proving that it was a great product. With my Kawasaki I'm getting power equal to anything I've ever had, also with the manufacturer's ECU on. That unit costs about £1,200, whereas an aftermarket unit costs about £6,000. If people have got £6,000 to blow on that unit, then let them, it's up to the individual. What I'm getting at is the cost of running the engine. If you tune that engine and need to keep it up to that level, it's going to cost you a lot of money to keep it up to that standard. I don't think our class can survive with the rule in place that allows you to do anything you like to that engine. As sure as eggs are eggs, I'm not going to go out there with a standard engine because it's all that I can afford. Because I want to win, I will go to any lengths to put together the best engine I can, so that I can compete, but then I'm one of those who can't afford to compete all year round as a result. I'm sat at home most weekends, because I can't afford to go on the boat to go and ride my bike. I've got forty grand's worth of sidecar outfit that's sat there doing nothing! It's all down to the amount of money my sponsors and I put in to the thing – if we weren't putting so much dough into the engine, we would be able to afford to go off and ride the thing. But we can't.

I think there is a lack of interest in general in sidecar racing from the outside world, which is a shame, because even today I still think that sidecars are way underestimated as a spectacle. It used to be that the sidecar TT would get two or three pages in *MotorCycle News*, back when I started out. Now you are lucky if it's a paragraph! The

TT organizers will insist that the Senior TT is the so–called 'blue riband' event, and that this is the race that everyone comes to watch. Well, I will argue till I hit my grave that it isn't. A good chunk of TT spectators will tell you that they are more interested in watching sidecars. I was asked by the TT organizing committee, in either 2002 or 2003, how I would feel if the sidecars were reduced to one race. I said that, to be perfectly honest, I would turn up for one race, but 90 per cent of the grid would not come here for two weeks for just one outing. I told them that if they were trying to cut a class, then look in another direction, because I'm sure that any readers' poll or viewers' poll will put the sidecars pretty near the top. I was told that this was once done by means of a tick sheet on the Isle of Man Steam Packet boats, and that the sidecars came out second. They made a point of ringing me and telling me, 'Yes, the sidecars came out near the top.' I said, 'Tell me how near?' They told me that sidecars were second behind the Senior TT. Well, I don't see that many people sitting on the hedge on Senior Race Day, because I'm one of them, and also there aren't that many bikes on the grid, because by the end of race week a lot of competitors have already gone home. The Formula One race on the Saturday is a popular event, but that's probably the high point of the week for solos.

If the rumours are true, that standard engines may be what's coming for this class, that's something which I tend to be in favour of, because I can budget to spend four to five thousand pounds on tuning an engine. That's *after* you've bought the engine in the first place, and that can cost you £2,000 to buy, so you can be looking at upwards of six grand to buy and tune an engine that can last five minutes. The costs come in the labour and the parts. We replace the gearbox with something that's more robust than the standard and also has a closer ratio. I personally like to replace standard con rods for an aftermarket con rod, then we have the crankshaft heat-treated and lightened, and balanced. We then have work done on pistons and cylinder heads, and replacement camshafts fitted. These changes are to make the parts stronger and more reliable. The easiest way to explain it to the guy watching from the side of the track is that a sidecar engine has to work a lot harder than a solo bike engine. That engine has to work twice as hard. For a start it has to push a bigger object through the air. It has a heavier object to drive along the road; it's got two men on it instead of one. It's doing twice the work. In data logging it has been shown that for a sidecar, for 70 per cent of a lap of the TT course, the throttle is wide open. Whereas on a 600cc solo, the throttle is open for 35 per cent of the lap, so it's double the work. That engine has to last for 114 miles, plus a couple of laps of practice with the throttle wide open for a long time. There is a lot more wear on a sidecar engine anyway, because of the oil sloshing about, though we can get round that with baffles in the sump, or a dry sump or whatever. But that isn't the biggest killer, it's the high revs and the fact that it's constant flat-out screaming that causes engines to fail. Then there are the other things that are going on in that engine. When you change down the gears, the load on the crankshaft reverses, and it puts thrust on the big end bearings. It really wears engine parts out fast. The rev counter on the dash tells you how fast the engine is going, and what temperature it's running at. There is a shift light built in on there, which tells you when to change gear without having to clock it. When it lights up it's time to click another gear. You could do it by feel but the light is quite intense and you can see it under the bodywork so it just makes it easier to know when to go up another gear. Another feature on a sidecar, which has been around for a long time but which was made compulsory a few years back, was the lanyard connected to the engine, which you attach to your leathers at some point. Then if you come flying off the thing it automatically kills the engine. I've spent a lot of time tweaking the position in which I put the engine. The distance between front wheel spindle and crankshaft centre can vary from 25 to 27 inches. A lot depends on the weight and height of the engine, so again you need to know which manufacturer's engine you are intending to use. The position of the engine can have an effect on the amount of understeer the outfit will suffer from. All outfits will suffer from it to a greater or lesser extent, but I think I've found a good compromise with the position of the engine, whereby I've reduced that understeer to a minimum. The passenger has a role to play in that as well, of course, and a good passenger can compensate for a lot. The other thing to bear in mind in this equation is the position of the driver's seat. You can make a lot of difference by moving it forwards or backwards, but I also put mine offset slightly towards the centre of the bike. It makes it slightly uncomfortable for riding but it does cope better going around left-handers.

I build the frame for the bike myself, and the engines are supplied by a manufacturer, but other parts are bought in as well. The wheels are cast in England at a foundry, and then spun up by an engineering shop that has big enough equipment to be able to do that. The wheels are specially made to my size and specifications; I have certain sized rims made and the wheel centres made in a certain way. The rims are pressed and spun as well. In setting up an outfit you can adjust the amount of 'toe-in' the sidecar wheel has. This is the amount by which the sidecar wheel turns in to point towards the front wheel of the bike. On a short circuit this can be pretty crucial, because the more 'toe-in' you have the easier it is to get round right-handers. At the TT, however, you would probably run the bike with no toe-in at all. On the long straight sections you don't want the thing constantly pulling to the right; I prefer it to be neutral if possible. The suspension units are hand-made in England. These are really important, actually, as a circuit like the TT mountain course is very bumpy in places. Sometimes when you hear a sidecar approaching, you can hear the revs going up and down as the rear wheel makes contact with the road and then loses it again because of the bumps. Apart from the negative effect it has on your speed to be losing contact with the road all the time, it's also very bad for the transmission and in particular for the chain. A lot of that problem can be sorted out with a decent set of shock-absorbers. I've worked a lot with Maxton, who produce these things, to come up with a really good system of shock-absorbers on my machines. For the same reason I also fit a steering damper; you don't have to use one on a sidecar outfit, but for the TT I think it takes a lot of the strain out of the steering, strain which comes from bouncing over those bumps. It makes it a bit more comfortable for me as well! I've tried different types of brakes, from different road bikes, and also precision-made brakes like you would see on World Superbikes or Moto GP. But I think the road-bike brakes are as good as you need for a sidecar. The other brakes don't seem to be any better for being a thousand pounds dearer! The handlebar brake is really there just as an emergency thing, because the rule book says it needs to be there. The footbrake really does the work, it operates the brakes on all three wheels. The braking ratio is 60:40, with most of the emphasis being on the front brakes. In fact you could probably run a sidecar with just a front brake, really, as it does vastly more work. There are two reservoirs for brake fluid located behind the fuel tank. One reservoir operates the callipers on the two front brake discs, the other serves the single callipers on each of the rear and sidecar wheels.

There are only two firms that make sidecar tyres. I was supported by Yokohama tyres for a long time, from 1993 up to 2008, but I fancied a change, it was as basic as that. A British company, Avon, have been making fantastic tyres for so many years, and I thought I would give them a try. I did in 2009 and we won the TT. I did have a deal with Yokohama where they supplied me with a couple of free sets for the TT and I carried their name on the bike, and likewise I have a similar deal now with Avon. The fairings I used to get for free in a sort of sponsorship deal. A guy used to supply bodywork to me for free and then he would advertise that I used them. Then in 2004 I decided that I wanted to do my own bodywork, so that it would be different from what everyone else was using. It took about a week of work and in materials maybe three hundred quid to produce the moulds for the bodywork that I'm still using today. I didn't even draw the thing, I just stood the sheets of aluminium up alongside the bike and plotted it out using a spirit level and a felt-tip pen. I took a level from various points, getting the contour that I wanted to follow. There's a 20 degree steering angle each way from central on the steering, meaning that it's a 40 degree sweep from left to right, so I made the nose of the bodywork just wide enough that it cleared the front wheel when it's on full lock. So I'd crudely made the shape that I wanted in aluminium, it looked roughly right, and from the inside of this thing I filled the corners up with bodyfiller and Plasticine. Then from this I made a fibreglass moulding called a plug, which is the shape that you ultimately want to achieve, from the inside of this thing. This plug was then 99 per cent the shape that I wanted, and the last 1 per cent I made up from more bodyfiller. Then I painted it as you would a car to give it a nice finish, and from that made the moulds from which I make all my bodywork today. The carbon fibre can be done in a vacuum but that's very expensive. I hand-lay all my stuff, which is just like a guy putting a fibreglass roof on your kitchen, it's that simple, almost. The principle is the same, although there's a finer aspect to the detail. I learned my fibreglass trade through boat-building with Freedom Yachts in the mid-1980s. I did maybe a year or eighteen months there, which taught me a lot about the bodywork side of things. The paintwork is done just like you would do on a car. I put a base coat on it, then put colours on while it's masked up. Then I put all my sponsors' names on it and finally give it a coat of clear lacquer after that. The fairing clips on to the chassis using Dzus fasteners, which were originally developed for the aviation industry. The front part of the fairing contains the air hose, channelling air from the air dam at the front. That links up with the airbox to force air into the engine.

A lot of people thought this body kit was crazy when I first went out with it. As always, there are different opinions on whether a thing is good or bad, whether it will work or not. It was just something that

I wanted to do, design this body kit out of my own head. I think some people tend to overanalyze things sometimes, debating the effect it will have on the airflow and so on. It really isn't that scientific, there's no magic formula, and as far as I'm concerned it will either work or it won't. At the end of the day it's just some plastic covering a three-wheeled object! There was also a lot of bullshit going around at the time that I'd had it designed in a wind tunnel, or that it was based on a Formula One car! Well, the nearest that thing got to a wind tunnel was the passageway outside my garage in Regaby with the north wind blowing! But after I had that crash in 2006 I even had people saying that they had told me that the bodywork was like an aerofoil or something, and that they knew I would take off with it sooner or later! In March 2006 the motorcycle side of Honda UK arranged a factory walkabout for me, at the Honda Formula One workshops at Banbury. It was interesting to see that the processes they used there for creating bodywork weren't a million miles away from the way I do things. They said to me that if I ever needed a job I should give them a ring!

Above all, though, my bikes are pretty basic things. There's no magic formula and no fancy bits that you can bolt on to make it go faster than anyone else; at the end of the day, as I always tell people when they buy an outfit from me, it's only as good on race day as the guy who is sitting on the seat and the guy who is kneeling next to him on the platform. After all, you could buy yourself a Stradivarius and it wouldn't make you a concert violinist, whereas Eric Clapton could probably get a decent tune out of a guitar that he bought in a second-hand shop ...

Notes

1. George O'Dell was born in Hemel Hempstead in 1945. In 1977 he became the first man on three wheels to lap the Isle of Man TT mountain circuit in excess of 100mph. He is notable for the fact that he achieved the title of World Champion in 1977 even though he had not won a single race, his consistency in achieving lower podium positions being enough to secure the title. It was ironic that the event he did win in 1977, the Isle of Man TT, had been stripped of World Championship points just the previous year. In 1981 O'Dell's difficulties in obtaining sponsorship, his marriage break-up, and some say his grief at the news of his friend Mike Hailwood's death, led him to take his own life by setting fire to his house after a stand–off with police.

2. German sidecar driver Rolf Steinhausen contested the TT between 1973 and 1981, winning three races. He was Sidecar World Champion in 1975 and 1976.

3. Born in 1951, Swiss sidecar racer Rolf Biland is noted for his innovation and experimental machines. Seven times World Champion, he competed at the TT between 1977 and 1980.

4. American Hall of Fame motorcyclist Dale Singleton was born in 1955. He began racing motorcycles at an early age in Georgia. A reporter overheard a friend refer to him as a pig farmer. The phrase stuck and he soon became known as 'The Flying Pig Farmer', a nickname he disliked, but one that actually brought him more notoriety as he raced in Europe. He was twice winner

of the Daytona 200 (1979 and 1981). He also won the 1981 AMA road race championship. He died in a private plane crash in 1985.

5. The Southern 100 road races were first run in 1955, with three races in the then 'traditional' classes: 250cc, 350cc, and the premier 500cc class. It was the first use of the 'Billown' circuit, a network of public roads around Castletown in the south of the Isle of Man. From an 'Open to Centre' status meeting in 1955, the Southern 100 gained National status in 1958 and was included in the British Championships in 1969. More recently the annual July event has been included in the prestigious Irish Regal Championships during 1992 and 1993 and has now gained European recognition.

6. Mick Boddice from Kidderminster in the West Midlands made his Isle of Man TT debut in 1966. His first win came in 1983 and he went on to win nine races at the TT. He now runs track days, teaching racing skills to newcomers.

7. Born in Pencaitland, East Lothian, Scottish sidecar racer John Robert 'Jock' Taylor electrified the three-wheeled world when he burst onto the scene in the late 1970s. He made his Isle of Man TT debut in 1978, and would win at the event four times in total. In 1980 he was crowned Sidecar World Champion. In 1981 he and passenger Benga Johansson took both races and smashed lap and race records. In 1982 in Race B Taylor and Johansson set a blistering pace, taking victory and setting a new sidecar lap record at the TT: 108.29mph. Later that same year, Taylor was killed while racing in wet conditions at the Finnish Grand Prix.

8. Carl Fogarty, MBE, from Blackburn, Lancashire, was four times World Superbike Champion. 'Foggy' began his racing career at the Isle of Man TT and was signed by Honda to ride in that event. He announced his departure from the TT in 1991, but returned to ride the Loctite Yamaha in 1992. His epic battle with Steve Hislop in the Senior that year has led to the race being

voted the 'greatest TT of all time' by fans. He was known for his horseplay while awaiting the start of a race.

9. Joey Dunlop, OBE, MBE, from Ballymoney in Northern Ireland, revered as the greatest TT racer of all time, scored a record twenty-six wins at the event. He won his last TT at the age of forty-eight in 2000. A few weeks later, Dunlop was killed in a crash while racing in Estonia.

10. Originally from St Helens, Colin Hardman made his home at Kirk Michael in the Isle of Man. He was killed in July 2006 while competing as a sidecar passenger at the Cock o' the North meeting at the Oliver's Mount, Scarborough circuit. Known to all as Cocker, he was widely respected and liked in racing circles.

11. Geoff Bell comes from a sidecar racing dynasty in the north-east of England. Both his father George (Geordie) Bell and his brother Ian raced sidecars. He was a double TT winner and lap record holder in 1992.

12. Rob Fisher from Cumbria was the winner of ten sidecar TT races between 1994 and 2002, second only to Dave Molyneux. He was also twice British Sidecar Champion.

13. Steve Hislop, known as 'Hizzy', from Hawick in Scotland, was one of the biggest TT stars of the 1980s and 1990s. Hislop scored eleven TT wins, his last being the 1994 Senior. He was twice British Superbike Champion. Hislop was killed in a helicopter crash in the Scottish borders in 2003.

14. Terry Windle is a former sidecar racer and arguably the best-known sidecar constructor in the sport. Between 1968 and 1980 he competed at the TT, but it was over a forty-year period as a constructor that he achieved his greatest success.

15. Darren Dixon, from Dover in Kent, began his racing career as a solo rider in the 1980s, enjoying considerable success. He later switched to three wheels and was twice Sidecar World Champion, in 1995 and 1996.

16. Steve Webster, MBE, was born in 1959. He began racing sidecars at club level aged nineteen. By 1983 he had moved up to World Championship level. He won his first World Championship in 1987 and went on to achieve a remarkable ten World Championship titles. He retired from racing in 2005.

17. Klaus Klaffenböck (nicknamed Klaffi) was born in 1968 in Peuerbach, Austria. He was Sidecar World Champion in 2001 and contested his first TT in 2005. He was winner of both sidecar races at the 2010 event.

18. John McGuinness, from Morecambe in Lancashire, was born in 1972. He began riding in motocross at the age of five and road racing at the age of eighteen. He won his first TT in 1999 and with fifteen TT wins to his name is the second most successful competitor in the history of the event. He currently rides for the HM Plant Honda team.

19. Manx-born Nick Crowe is the winner of five sidecar TT races. In 2008 he was British Sidecar Champion. Serious injuries received in the crash at the 2009 TT forced his retirement from sidecar racing.

20. Tim Reeves from Maidstone in Kent began racing sidecars in 1990 as a passenger. In 1999 he switched to driving. He was Sidecar World Champion in 2005, the first of three World Championships which Reeves has won.

Appendix I

Technical Drawings

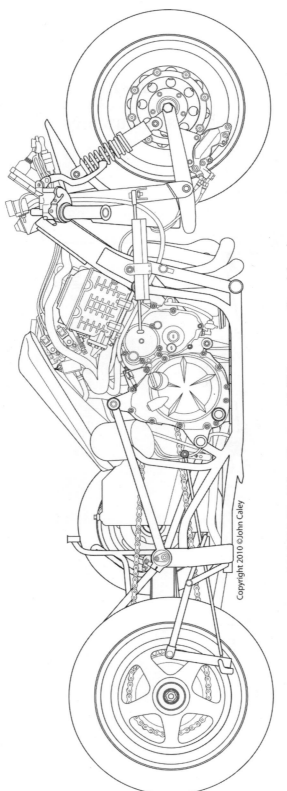

2010 DMR 600cc Kawasaki Sidecar outfit, side view.

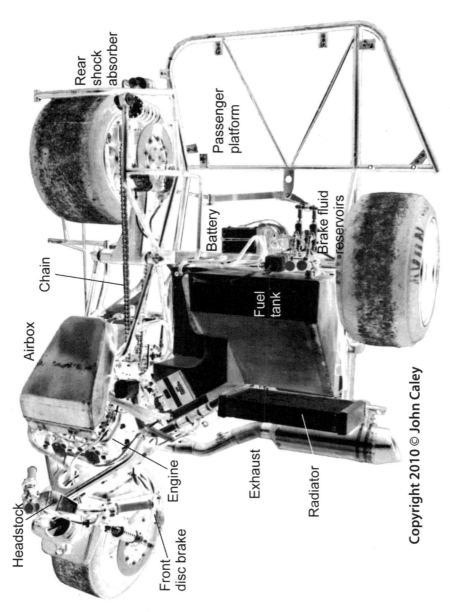

Rear shock absorber

Passenger platform

Battery

Brake fluid reservoirs

Chain

Fuel tank

Airbox

Headstock

Engine

Front disc brake

Exhaust

Radiator

Copyright 2010 © John Caley

2010 DMR 600cc Kawasaki Sidecar outfit, frame and layout.

Appendix II

Tables of Results (National level or above)

Isle of Man TT

Year	Race	Position
1987	Race A	10th
1988	Race A	6th
1989	Race A	1st
1989	Race B	3rd
1991	Race B	3rd
1992	Race A	6th
1992	Race B	3rd
1993	Race A	1st
1993	Race B	1st
1994	Race A	2nd
1994	Race B	2nd
1995	Race B	2nd
1996	Race A	1st
1996	Race B	1st
1998	Race B	1st
1999	Race A	1st
2002	Race A	4th
2002	Race B	2nd
2003	Race B	1st
2004	Race A	1st
2004	Race B	1st
2005	Race B	1st
2007	Race A	1st
2007	Race B	1st
2008	Race B	2nd
2009	Race A	1st
2010	Race A	2nd

Ulster Grand Prix

Year	Position
1995	1st

British Championship races

Year	Race	Position
1988	Donington Park	4th
1988	Carnaby	6th
1993	Brands Hatch	3rd
1993	Oulton Park	2nd
1994	Donington Park	2nd
1994	Knockhill	5th
1994	Oulton Park	1st
1994	Brands Hatch	1st
1996	Silverstone	4th
1996	Donington Park	6th
2006	Brands Hatch	1st
2006	Cadwell Park	1st

Southern 100

Year	Race	Position
1984	Consolation Race	2nd
1985	Consolation Race	1st
1986	Race 1	1st
1986	Race 2	1st
1987	Race 1	2nd
1987	Race 2	2nd
1988	Race 1	2nd
1988	Race 2	2nd
1991	Race 1	1st
1991	Race 2	1st
1992	Race 1	3rd

1992	Race 2	1st
1993	Race 1	1st
1993	Race 2	1st
1994	Race 1	1st
1995	Race 1	1st
1998	Race 1	2nd
1998	Race 2	1st
1999	Race 1	1st
2002	Race 1	1st
2002	Race 2	1st
2003	Race 2	1st

European Championship races

Year	Race	Position
1995	Assen, Holland	6th
1995	Donington, England	3rd
1996	Vallelunga, Italy	2nd
1996	Schleiz, Germany	1st
1996	Catalonia, Spain	12th
2002	Assen, Holland	1st

World Championship races

Year	Race	Position
1996	Brno, Czech Republic	6th
1997	Hungaroring, Hungary	6th
1997	A1 Ring, Austria	7th
2000	Hockenheim, Germany	5th
2007	Brands Hatch, England	9th
2007	Schleiz, Germany	11th
2007	Salzburgring, Austria	12th
2007	Rijeka, Croatia	6th
2007	Le Mans, France	6th

TT Races won as a constructor

Year	Race	Driver
1993	Race A	Dave Molyneux
1993	Race B	Dave Molyneux
1995	Race A	Rob Fisher
1995	Race B	Rob Fisher
1996	Race A	Dave Molyneux
1996	Race B	Dave Molyneux
1998	Race B	Dave Molyneux
1999	Race A	Dave Molyneux
2002	Race A	Rob Fisher
2002	Race B	Rob Fisher
2003	Race A	Ian Bell
2003	Race B	Dave Molyneux
2004	Race A	Dave Molyneux
2004	Race B	Dave Molyneux
2005	Race A	Nick Crowe
2005	Race B	Dave Molyneux
2006	Race A	Nick Crowe
2006	Race B	Nick Crowe
2007	Race A	Dave Molyneux
2007	Race B	Dave Molyneux
2009	Race A	Dave Molyneux

Index